Making the SHIFT Field Guide

Implementing the Three Big Shifts from SHIFT: Three Big Moves for the 21st Century Church

Mark E. Tidsworth

CONTENTS

INTRODUCTION

"And in praying do not heap up empty phrases as the Gentiles do; for they think that they will be heard for their many words. Do not be like them, for your Father knows what you need before you ask him. Pray then like this:

> Our Father who art in heaven, Hallowed be thy name.
> Thy kingdom come, Thy will be done, On earth as it is in heaven.
> Give us this day our daily bread; And forgive us our debts, As we also have forgiven our debtors; And lead us not into temptation, But deliver us from evil. For thine is the kingdom, and the power, and the glory forever, Amen."

Matthew 6:7-13

Evidently we don't need a lot of words to convince God of our needs. It's not like we need to lay out a sophisticated rationale, demonstrating our need is sufficient for divine

1

intervention, in order for God to hear and respond. No, God is more like a loving parent; eager to engage God's children, happy they are bringing the important cares and concerns of their lives.

This short prayer (above) is how Jesus taught his disciples to pray. In fact, he warned against long prayers; at least the type designed to gain attention for ourselves from others besides God. Instead Jesus encourages brevity and simplicity. It's like he's saying, "Just get to the point without all the posturing and attention-seeking."

Disciples of Jesus Christ have used this model for praying for centuries in every corner of our planet. The words are well-worn, repeated so many times every day that none of us could keep count (only God knows and it's not for our ears anyway).

But I wonder....I wonder about this phrase right in the middle of this model prayer: "Thy kingdom come, thy will be done, on earth as it is in heaven." Wow. Does this mean what we think it might mean? In recent years, this Lord's Prayer statement has taken hold of me. My relationship to this statement is not static, shifting over time. In this one statement there are depths of spiritual insight into which only my big toe is immersed. Sophisticated scholars can provide deep theological truths regarding the Lord's Prayer, yet I would offer these thoughts for your consideration.

First, this prayer calls us to pray for God's kingdom to come on earth.
(Stating the obvious, yet overlooked)
Who can adequately describe God's kingdom in all its rich

diversity, depth, and power? The clues we find in scripture describe a kingdom bringing healing, restoration, reconciliation, peace, justice, mercy, love, hope, etc. Nearly everything good, blessed, healthy, and whole has its origin in God and God's kingdom. The kingdom is about putting a world gone mad into its right mind. It's about bringing goodness to our brokenness. It's about a world worth inhabiting.

So, Jesus, in this model prayer, encourages us to pray this kingdom of God will happen here (on earth), just like it does there (in heaven). Given this, one would believe that Jesus himself believed God's kingdom coming on earth like it is in heaven is actually a real possibility.

I can remember so many sermons and Bible study lessons wherein the preacher or teacher described this world's destiny as a huge conflagration in one fiery ball. That doesn't sound much like God's kingdom coming on earth as it is in heaven. So, was Jesus just teasing us? Did Jesus want to give us some hope to live by, even though he knew God would burn this planet in the end? Was this just a way to occupy disciples until God and the angels could come and rescue the saints before destroying the sinners?

Over time, through must perspective shifting, I've come to believe that Jesus intended to bring God's kingdom to earth (and still does). His life, ministry, teachings, death, and resurrection were the inaugural acts in this kingdom drama. Now his followers (us) are called to collaborate with God's mission of kingdom actualization. Just like it is in heaven...that's the kind of world Jesus wants for this planet.

What audacity, what a dreamer, what a calling...
Now, how much will we collaborate and partner with God around God's mission to bring the kingdom to earth as it is in heaven?

Transformation
"This world is not what it was intended to be, nor is it yet what it shall be."
Dr. William Hendrix, my seminary theology professor, was fond of this saying. We live in the in-between time. This world is evolving, changing, shifting, moving – and we along with it. So, as we move along we are being transformed, while the world is being transformed. When we cooperate and collaborate with God, we are changed. We become different people than we were. This radical Lord's Prayer holds within it a call to transformation.

This Field Guide is a tool for engaging ourselves in kingdom process. We are called to participate with God's hopes and dreams for our world, which include transformation. Specifically, the purpose of this Field Guide is to provide spiritual direction for those of us who want to make the personal and faith community shifts necessary to partner with God.

More specifically, this Field Guide is designed to give opportunity to you and your small group to collectively pursue the answers to three questions. These three questions are behind the three big moves described in *Shift: Three Big Moves For The 21st Century Church.* They are listed here, with their connection to the three movements we are pursuing in our personal and faith community experience.

What does it mean to be a disciple of Jesus Christ?

Member Identity to Disciple Identity

What does it mean to be disciples who join God on mission in the world?

Attractional Church to Missional Church

What does it mean to be in partnership with disciples who join God on mission in the world?

Consumer Culture to Sacred Partnering

If you've read the Shift book, you may notice these questions themselves have shifted from what's in the book. We are rearranging their order in this Field Guide so that we can connect them more sequentially to these three big moves.

SMALL GROUP GATHERING FORMAT

Using the following format for each small group gathering will build continuity, while facilitating the group engaging these Shifts in a proactive way. Here's what the format looks like, along with a word of explanation for group leaders.

Each Small Group Gathering – *1 Hour*
Leaders are encouraged to adjust the time spent in each aspect depending on your context. In other words, the times below are suggestions. Adapt them as needed.

Gathering – *15 Minutes*
Bringing ourselves, gathering ourselves to any significant experience takes intentionality. When the group leader starts this gathering activity, it helps disciples focus on being together in the spirit of Christ. Each gathering experience will be different, connected in some way to the theme of that particular small group gathering.

Praying – *10 Minutes*
The same prayer is provided for each small group gathering. Engaging prayer in this liturgical-like way will help the group gather, and find its rhythm. Either select someone beforehand to lead this prayer, or the group leader can lead. There's opportunity for spontaneous praying included.

Engaging – *20 Minutes*
Our purpose here is to engage God, ourselves, and one another in learning and growth. Sometimes new material is introduced, requiring some reading during the group experience. Other times, sharing from the previous week's engagements is the focus. Small group leaders will find instructions in these engagements as needed, while many are self-explanatory.

Previewing – *5 Minutes*
Here the group leader previews the coming week's engagements. We encourage small group leaders to secure a copy of *Shift: Three Big Moves For The 21st Century Church*, reading it for an expanded understanding of this content. Leaders use these minutes to describe the Shift theme coming for the week, preparing the group to engage each day.

Harvesting – *10 Minutes*
For years, I've been using a practice at the end of retreats, Bible studies, Coaching groups and basically any small group gathering. We simply ask disciples to verbalize what they gained from this experience. This practice brings laser-focus to insights which are drifting through our minds. When disciples verbalize their insights, among these witnesses, they harvest them for their benefit. Another benefit is the

inspiration we gain as we listen to our spiritual kin share their insights. You will find this activity mutually beneficial.

Sending – *2 Minutes*
We are the Church, gathered at times and dispersed at others. Our calling includes joining God on mission in the world. Sending is a way to launch us out into God's world, having been renewed through this small group gathering. There will be some variety in format. Leaders, read ahead and plan how to facilitate this part of the small group gathering.

Identifying Our Agreements
When I lead coaching groups, we identify our agreements as we begin. I learned to do this way back in graduate school for therapists. We were learning to do group counseling. We discovered that the structure placed around and below a group directly influenced the level of sharing which would occur. Sloppy structure = minimal sharing and therapeutic work. Confidentiality, participation, showing up, and speaking only for oneself were significant practices requiring specific attention. Now that I lead coaching groups, I continued this agreement-making practice. We don't need as many agreements as therapeutic groups, yet sufficient agreements make for a robust experience.

So, what about this small group experience? What agreements may be helpful to you? You don't want unnecessary or overly-detailed agreements which become burdensome and hinder more than help. Simultaneously, you do want helpful practices which help everyone engage this growth opportunity with confidence and eagerness.

Here are potential agreements for you to consider as you

begin.

We will do our best to:

- Be spiritually, relationally and physically present for each small group gathering
- Participate; making our contributions to this small group for the benefit of the group
- Respect each other by not interrupting, listening attentively, and honoring the perspectives of one another
- Avoid taking too much air time for myself, while also not withholding my input

CONNECTING AND ORIENTING

Gathering

Do you know everyone in this group? What a great opportunity to deepen ongoing relationships while connecting with new friends. As you begin today, do a go around, giving each person an opportunity to introduce themselves. You might share things like your name, how long you have lived in this community, how long you have been part of this church, family relationships and work life. Do make sure you fill in this statement: "I decided to participate in this small group because _____."

Praying

Leader: We recognize, O God, that you were here before we arrived.

Group: We recognize, O God, that you are with us at all times, in all places.

Leader: Even before we made our way here, even before we moved through this day,

Group: You were here, waiting, anticipating our gathering in this place.

Leader: For you delight in your children, O God.
Group: When we gather in your name and in your Spirit, you rejoice.
Leader: So now, we also rejoice in you. We reflect on our lives this week and bring these items of gratitude to you, in the presence of these sisters and brothers in Christ:
(As you are moved, speak your gratitude aloud. As others share, silently lift their gratitude to God)

Leader: And now, O God, we also bring our concerns, as your children, to you as our loving heavenly parent:
(As you are moved, speak your concern aloud. As others share, silently lift their concerns to God)

Leader: And now, O God, we give you thanks for this opportunity to engage each other in life's pilgrimage.
Group: We ask that you fill us with your Holy Spirit and wrap this experience in your love.
All: Through the grace, power and love of Jesus Christ our Lord, may it be so. Amen.

Our Agreements
Look over the agreements in the Introduction. Briefly discuss which and what agreements might help your small group function well. Space is provided here for recording them. You might narrow them down to one word or a phrase, like "participate" or "show-up."

_____

_____

_____

Engaging

> "The kingdom of heaven is like treasure hidden in a
> field, which someone found and hid; then in his joy
> he goes and sells all that he has and buys that field.
> Again, the kingdom of heaven is like a merchant in
> search of fine pearls; on finding one pearl of great
> value, he went and sold all that he had and bought
> it."

Matthew 16:44-46

> "O taste and see that the Lord is good; happy are
> those who take refuge in him."

Psalm 34:8

(Either the group leader will read aloud the following
thoughts, or take turns reading a paragraph aloud)
Jesus' parables....
Stories, pithy sayings, brief truths which illuminate the
pathway to life.
This kingdom of heaven thing; this kingdom of God....when
we sample even a small taste or catch a brief glimpse, we are
captivated. When we taste of the Lord, we find that the Lord
is good.

Then, we are willing to give up everything for life in this
kingdom. We are like the moths circling the back porch light
on a pleasant summer evening – we just can't stay away from
this kingdom. When we experience something of the
kingdom, we are captivated by Christ and will do most
anything to experience God even more.

Paradoxically, this is what it takes to experience the kind of
life described as the Way of Jesus. As it turns out, losing is

finding. In varying places in the gospels, we find Jesus describing this paradoxical faith journey.

> Then Jesus told his disciples, "If any want to become my followers, let them deny themselves and take up their cross and follow me. For those who want to save their life will lose it, and those who lose their life for my sake will find it. For what will it profit them if they gain the whole world but forfeit their life? Or what will they give in return for their life?"
>
> *Matthew 16: 24-26*

As strange as it seems, we find life (significant, genuine, authentic, joyous) by letting go. The very opposite of how we intuitively might seek to find life leads to life...letting go, releasing, giving over in faith. When we trust God with our lives, relinquishing the belief that we can manage life ourselves; that's when life begins.

This is so counter-cultural, so radically different than nearly every message we receive from the world around us. We are taught that the aggressive and assertive will get ahead; that we must go out and make life happen. Isn't it ironic that real life actually begins when we reach the end of our competency? When we recognize our limitations and give ourselves over to God...that's when we find that pearl of great price.

One of our ordinances or sacraments (depending on your particular denominational branch on this Christian family tree) is baptism. Those denominations who practice the immersion mode of baptism watch this spiritually-based drama unfold each time a new disciple is baptized. One enters the water and then is lowered down beneath the water, symbolizing entering the tomb and dying to self. Then, one is raised from the water, symbolizing resurrection to new life. This dramatic ordinance or sacrament which the Christian Church has practiced for centuries visually "acts-out" this process of dying and rising.

Previewing

This is our theme for Week One of this Making The Shift experience; dying to self and rising to Christ. Each of the six Daily Engagements for this week explore and expand this theme. Actually, this is the crux of salvation; giving ourselves over to God. Do you remember when Jesus was in the Garden of Gethsemane, looking over into the next day when he would face the ordeal of the cross? Though he prepared for these moments throughout his ministry, now he's struggling with the reality before him. Ultimately, he moves to the place of spiritual resolution, praying, "Father, not my will be done, but thy will be done." Then he was ready. Jesus gave himself to God's calling for his life. May we model our lives after our ultimate Model, Jesus Christ our Lord.

Next week's Small Group Gathering will include reflection on some of the week's Daily Engagements.

Harvesting

Silently reflect on all you have experienced today in this small group. Listen to your heart, spirit, mind for what stands out – for what may be God's word for you right now. As you listen and reflect, allow the single insight which you need to rise to your awareness.

Go around the group, inviting each disciple to share what

he/she has gained from this experience.

As always, sharing is optional. This is a "no shame" group. As people share their insight, others are invited to listen with support, receiving and respecting the spiritual process of others (without commenting).

Sending

Now, as you go, know that you ARE God's people.

God's creative Spirit brought you into this world.

God's power sustains you to this very moment.

So go now, and be who you are in Christ.

Go as salt, to flavor this world. Go as light, to shine in the darkness.

Go as grace, to bring healing and hope to this broken and hurting world.

And may the peace of God, which surpasses all comprehension, guard our hearts and minds in Christ Jesus until we meet again.

Amen.

Daily Engagements
Dying and Rising

Dying And Rising – Day One

Why you?
Why you as a disciple of Jesus Christ?
What is it about the Father, Son, and Holy Spirit that you choose to follow?
What is it about this Christian movement that influences you to be a Christ follower?

Most of us become Christ followers due to the influence of many persons and circumstances. We come to faith in such varied ways. But now, you are invited to consider what it is which influences you to follow Jesus Christ as a disciple now....during this season of your life. You could conceivably be a part of any other world religion. You could have walked away from your faith in Christ. You could have simply drifted away from your identity as a disciple. Instead, here you are, doing this Daily Engagement, investing in your faith journey. There is something about the Lord God which draws you, perhaps even captivates you. Could it be the pearl of great price or the treasure found in a field? Just what is it about living in the Way of Jesus Christ which captivates you?

_____
_____
_____
_____
_____

Praying
O God, you have drawn me to you, even when I had no idea what was happening. Today I thank you for including me in your great love. I pray that today you will shape me into an instrument of your grace. Help me to reflect the kind of love

you showed me as I engage others. May I be who you have called me to be this very day.

Sending
As you go today, remember what it is that draws you into this Christian Movement. Consider how you can actualize (live it) this today.

Dying And Rising – Day Two

Another way to phrase this spiritual process is letting go and taking hold. We are called to let go of our self-focused lives, recognizing Jesus Christ as Lord of life, and then taking hold of a spiritual pilgrimage called discipleship. Then we follow, becoming one of those people who live in the Way of Jesus (see Acts). This is the process of salvation; shedding layers and layers of cultural and spiritual brokenness while layering on new attitudes, beliefs, and behaviors. A new way of life emerges as we engage this life of faith.

Trapeze artists demonstrate great trust. They trust their partners to be there to catch them as they fly through space toward outstretched hands. In order to execute this flight, this high-flying acrobat must be willing to let go of his/her swing. There is no way to complete this maneuver without first letting go. Sufficient and actionable trust must be present. This acrobat is willing to trade safety on the swing for free flight given the potential gains, trusting this move will lead to something very desirable.

For we disciples of Jesus Christ, this leads us to the trust question: "Do we trust God?"
Our tendency is to quickly answer, "Yes, of course."
Then the follow up, more focused question comes to us: "Enough to let go of our trapeze?"
In other words, how much do we trust God?

This is our calling – trusting God with our lives.

Praying
You are invited to ask God what holds you back when it comes to trusting God.

Sending
If we had the faith of a tiny mustard seed, we could move mountains. Go forth today, believing God will give you the faith you need to do what God calls you to do this very day.

Dying And Rising – Day Three

The Preface to Shift describes the author's struggle with finding God in the institutional church. Family crises, church dislocation, and ministerial angst conspired to bring a dark time of searching to his life. This valley pilgrimage included wondering if he could connect with the church-as-he-had-experienced-it again. His relationship to the church included a very clear dis-ease.

Have you ever been there? Too many Christ-followers are walking away from church in this postmodern age. Evidently, plenty of people are struggling with their relationship with church-as-we-have-known-it. How do you relate to the disconnect some disciples describe between their understandings of Jesus Christ and their experience with church? How does this personally relate to you?

_____

_____

_____

_____

_____

Praying
Based on your answers above, what is your prayer today? Honestly bring yourself to God, who cares for you like a parent with a dear child.

Sending
Lay aside the baggage which holds you down. Go with the assurance that you are loved, and called to be an instrument of God's grace this very day.

Dying And Rising – Day Four

Three questions saved the author's (spiritual) life.
What does it mean to be a disciple of Jesus Christ?
What does it mean to be a gathered community of disciples?
*What does it mean to be a gathered community of disciples
who join God on mission in the world?*
These questions captivated the author's attention, becoming
driving questions for his life.

In reality, our lives answer the questions we find most
compelling.
When we observe our lives, we can see that we are in the
process of answering life's questions by the way we go about
our living. What we do, how we use our time, our
relationships, our discretionary time...all these are answers to
the questions of our lives. We are demonstrating by our living
what we believe makes for the kind of life we want to live.

So what are they? What are the questions which your life's
activities are answering? What is the bottom line question(s)
for you? As objectively and honestly as you can, look at your
life and discern what questions are driving you.

_____

_____

_____

_____

_____

Dying to self and rising to Christ is our theme this week.
Reflecting on your answers above, what might need to go the
way of all things (dying)? What might be taking up room in
your life, but no longer reflects your spiritual journey as a

disciple? And then, how might your refine the questions you are pursuing? What new questions are rising up for you?

_____

_____

_____

_____

_____

Praying
You are invited to pray that God will de-clutter your life. God is not pushy, forcing discipleship. Instead, God waits for your invitation.

Sending
Go forward today in faith, believing and trusting that God is providing all the spiritual power you need to move through whatever challenges present themselves.

Dying And Rising – Day Five

Just like individual disciples, churches also answer their important questions. We can look at the list of activities to find clues about what any particular church believes is important. The expectations communicated by the church also help us identify the important questions. Reflect on your experience of your faith community. What appears very important to your church? What are the questions your faith community is trying to answer with its activities?

_____

_____

_____

_____

Dying to self and rising to Christ is our theme this week. There are times to lay aside what is no longer relevant, or what holds us back from following Christ. Reflecting on your church, what may need to be discontinued or at least reformed?

_____

_____

_____

_____

_____

Praying

Humility. Whenever we believe we are humble, we are the slippery slope toward pride. Humility involves recognizing our flawed existence, even while we try following God's call. Pray for your church today with humility. Hold your answers to the queries above up to God in a spirit of humility, knowing your personal discernment is flawed. This will help you relate graciously with those who are part of your faith community.

Sending
You don't go to church. You ARE the Church. In the clear awareness and assurance of who you are, live today as the Church sent into God's world.

Dying And Rising – Day Six

"I give you a new commandment, that you love one
another. Just as I have loved you, you should also
love one another. By this everyone will know that
you are my disciples, if you have love for one
another."

John 13:34-35, NSRV

I have received a few criticisms and a couple observations
about the use of this New Commandment. One person
offered the perspective that the Great Commandment would
be better, since it parallels the Great Commission (Matthew
28:18-20) to which I also referred in the book's Introduction. I
appreciate the criticism, since it informs me that people are
reading thoughtfully. Also, this drove me to reflect. Why did
Jesus, as recorded in John's gospel, give this New
Commandment? It seems he might have again quoted the
Shema as he did when asked which commandment is
greatest (Gospel of Matthew).

The context of John 13 is the Farewell Discourse. Jesus is
readying himself and the disciples for the ordeal of the
crucifixion and miracle of the resurrection. It's like this is his
last chance to give last minute instructions on what's
important. So, why introduce this New Commandment in his
last discourse? Why the emphasis on loving one another,
identifying this as the test by which the world will know we
are disciples?

_____

_____

_____

Praying

There are people in this world who need love....not from just anyone, but from you. Consider asking God who needs loved by you today, committing yourself to doing so.

Sending

Faith, hope, and love; these three abide. But the greatest of these is love.

Go forth as an expression of God's great love for this world.

HARVESTING DYING AND RISING

Gathering

Play the Name Game: The first person in the circle shares his first name, the second repeats the first's name and then states her name. The third person repeats the first two names, adding his. Continue around the circle with the leader going last, reciting everyone's first name. This is a fun way to help the group know names.

Take a moment to see if anyone has news (pleasant or unpleasant) which he/she wants the group to know from this week.

Praying

Leader: We recognize, O God, that you were here before we arrived.

Group: We recognize, O God, that you are with us at all times, in all places.

Leader: Even before we made our way here, even before we moved through this day,

Group: You were here, waiting, anticipating our gathering in this place.

Leader: For you delight in your children O God.

Group: When we gather in your name and in your Spirit, you rejoice.

Leader: So now, we also rejoice in you. We reflect on our lives this week and bring these items of gratitude to you, in the presence of these sisters and brothers in Christ:

(As you are moved, speak your gratitude aloud. Pray your gratitude to God as others share)

Leader: And now, O God, we also bring our concerns, as your children, to you as our loving heavenly parent:

(As you are moved, speak your concern aloud. As you hear others share, pray their concerns to God)

Leader: And now, O God, we give you thanks for this opportunity to engage each other in life's pilgrimage.

Group: We ask that you fill us with your Holy Spirit and wrap this experience in your love.

All: Through the grace, power and love of Jesus Christ our Lord, may it be so. Amen.

Engaging

Engage with each other around Day 6 from this week's Daily Engagements:

1. Why this one? Why this New Commandment in the Farewell Discourse? What might Jesus be trying to communicate here?

2. Given this New Commandment's relevance, how might it inform and shape our lives?

3. There are many actions Jesus did not recommend for changing (improving) this world (political control, military intervention, dominating others, etc.). Jesus did emphasize loving one another. Just how powerful is love? Powerful enough to transform the world? And, just how does that work?

Daily Engagement Day 1 – You were asked to reflect on your faith journey.
What is it about living in the Way of Jesus which captivates you? Why do you choose to be a part of this Christian movement in the world? Do a go around, inviting each person to share about their engagement with this daily engagement. (Remember that sharing is always optional).

Previewing
Change has always been around. What's different now is the pace of change. Watch the video, entitled "Did You Know?" found on you tube from the link below. A new "Did You Know" is produced each year (I like this one from 2011 because of its great music!)
https://www.youtube.com/watch?v=F9WDtQ4Ujn8
(Leader, use whatever mode of technology you have available to show this video – a screen, TV, your laptop, etc.)

Like we mentioned, change is not new. The pace of change is different; exponential in particular.
Most changes bring gains and losses. Discuss what losses you see and experience in our society, given the technological and cultural advances since the year 2000. Then, discuss the gains you see and experience in our society, given the advances

identified above.

> "...that with the Lord one day is like a thousand years,
> and a thousand years are like one day."
>
> *2 Peter 3:8*

Knowing this, that God's view of time is different than our view of time, what does this awareness do for you as a disciple as you engage this rapidly changing world in which we live? (Discuss)

This week, you will engage learning focused on major shifts in North American culture, plus in the Church.

Harvesting

As you listened to your spiritual relatives share their insights during this Small Group, what are you learning or gaining which will strengthen you as a disciple? Fill in the blank at the end of this sentence, "Something I've gained from this experience is _____."

Sending

(Based on Micah 6:8)

Leader: And what is it Lord that you require?

Group: To do justice, helping this world move toward what is good and healthy.

Leader: And what else O Lord do you require?

Group: To love kindness, for this world is hungry and thirsty for compassionate engagement.

Leader: And how shall we relate to you O God?

Group: Walking humbly with you O God, knowing we are your children, living securely as one of your beloved.

Leader: Sisters and brothers, let's make it so!

Group: Praise be to God!

Daily Engagements
Contexting

Contexting – Day One

"One very cold night a group of porcupines huddled together for warmth. However, their spines made proximity uncomfortable, so they moved apart again and got cold. After shuffling repeatedly in and out, they eventually found a distance at which they could still be comfortably warm without getting pricked. This distance they henceforth called decency and good manners."

E.O. Wilson
Sociobiology: The New Synthesis, 1975

I've enjoyed E. O. Wilson's parable about how culture develops for a long time. Laughter typically erupts when people see it for the first time. Some may remember the old joke about how to cook a ham, which also describes how cultural norms develop (email if you don't know it). Every group of people develop a micro-culture among them over time, using that culture to guide their interactions and activities. This is normal and natural, neither positive nor negative. This is simply how human beings relate in groups.

Faith communities also develop their unique culture over time. Imagine for a moment you are completely unfamiliar with how your faith community functions. You show up alone for worship. You walk in with no knowledge of how things work here, equipped with only your interest in worshipping God and connecting with people. What would you need to learn in order to participate with worship? How steep is the learning curve? Are people ready and waiting to help you participate? Where are the open doors which invite you into

37

the culture of this faith community?

_____

_____

_____

Praying

Pray that God will help you and your faith community to form a culture of Christian hospitality. Pray for more open doors to your faith community. Pray for yourself as a disciple who contributes to and shapes the culture of your faith community.

Sending

Today look for one door which you can open to another person who may be left out of a group. May you function as a "holy bellman," opening the door and welcoming people inside.

Contexting – Day Two

Changing and shifting culture is not new. Change has been in play since the beginning of time. What's new about change is its speed. The speed of change is now exponential. Phyllis Tickle (historian) provides great insight for us about large-scale cultural changes to which the Church responds (more in the Shift book). She cleverly uses the metaphor of a rummage sale, describing what's happening in her book *The Great Emergence* (2008). About every 500 years, the Church clears out its attic, holding a rummage sale. The sign out front reads, "Everything must go." Tickle traces these major shifts in the life of the Church including:

•   30-70AD – Birth of the church – 70-130: decline of Judaism

•   590AD (or so) – Fall of the Roman Empire and Beginning of the Dark Ages

•   1054AD – The Great Schism – Church divided between East and West

•   1517 (or so) – The Great Reformation and Beginning of The Modern Period

•   2000 + - Post-Modern Period

The result of this Rummage Sale experience is that we are living in a new era. Again we are unsure of what to call it, simply knowing it is "Post" what was before.

This means that church-as-we-have-known-it is going the way of all things. We do not mean the Church itself is going away. Instead we mean that the way churches have expressed and organized themselves is changing. Now, newer, culturally renovated expressions of Church are emerging.

Praying

How do you feel about these insights...the awareness that church-as-we-have-know-it is shifting? We are highly unlikely to return to the 1950s way of being church (nor the 1980s, or even 2000s). What emotions, thoughts, reflections rise up in you as this awareness rises? Today you are invited to bring your reactions to God in prayer. Some will find it helpful to write out your internal prayer dialogue with God. Others might speak quietly out loud about this. In whatever way fits for you, engage God around these shifts in the way we are church.

Sending

You ARE the church. Through Christ, God is making everything new. So, today look for the newness God is creating in the church through you.

Contexting – Day Three

In the year 300 CE, Emperor Constantine declared Christianity
to be the "official" religion of the Empire (Rome). Since then,
the Christian faith and governments in Europe and now North
America have danced together. Now, in North America, the
Christian movement is falling out of favor with the Empire
(state) and becoming less culturally affirmed. Christian
disciples are finding themselves in cultural positions more like
the early days of our faith, when the Christian movement was
counter-cultural.

Ever since I can remember (born 1962), Christianity has been
in a favored, majority position in this country (USA). Now that
Christianity is moving toward minority status, cultural shifts
are afoot. What signs do you see that Christianity is no longer
reinforced or affirmed by the larger culture around you?

_____

_____

_____

During times of significant change, there is danger and
opportunity inherent in the shifts. For the Christian
movement, what dangers and opportunities are these cultural
shifts presenting to God's Church?

Dangers: _____

_____

Opportunities: _____

_____

Praying

Every day there are opportunities to grow in our faith and as persons. Consider asking God to expand who you are as a person and disciple today. Consider asking God to help you notice these growth opportunities as they present themselves.

Sending

God provides everything we need to do what God calls us to do.

Go forth today, knowing you are equipped for every good work.

No fear; no hesitation.

Contexting – Day Four

Changes in our Postmodern Culture:
- The pace of change is exponential
- Distrust for organizations is on the rise, while loyalty to organizations is declining
- There is low toleration for meaningless activities (like unproductive meetings)
- We are part of the global economy, experiencing more ups and downs than before
- Spiritual sensitivity and hunger are on the rise
- There is a strong desire among many to make a positive difference in the world
- The digital divide is growing
- Weekly worship attendance is declining
- Increasing numbers of Americans do not identify with any faith community
- The place of church and clergy is less central to the life of communities

> From the Introduction to
> *Disciple Development Coaching*
> Mark Tidsworth and Ircel Harrison

Various names for church appear in this Field Guide, like "Christian movement" and "faith community." These names or phrases suggest a more fluid, action-oriented understanding of church. During these Postmodern times in which we find ourselves, organizations of all kinds are undergoing transformation, with the church as no exception.

All the shifts considered so far mean that the Christian Church is becoming more of a movement than many of us have experienced before. We are moving away from self-identifying as organizations or community institutions to a movement of the Spirit or a faith community of disciples. We may continue to use buildings and organizational structures, but we are being driven to identify and pursue the essence of our faith...living as disciples of Jesus who join God on mission in the world.

Praying
How fluid is your faith? In other words, how much is your faith alive and growing? Consider discussing this with God now.

Sending
God is on the move...creating, renewing, reconciling. Look for God's movement in the places you are today, joining God's mission in your context.

Contexting – Day Five

All of us are trying to make sense of the cultural shifts around us in relation to our faith. This is natural and normal when change comes our way. Individual disciples and churches are responding to the large scale shifts in the culture of North America. Where are you in relation to these large scale shifts? How are the large scale shifts affecting your faith journey? Consider the reactions and responses below, identifying which cluster describes your current stage of development.

Cluster One - Defensive Reactions
When we realize large scale change is here, and that it impacts our lives, forcing us to give up previous ways of functioning, we react. Often we engage in a cluster of reactions which are not very helpful, yet they represent our first or early responses to change.

- Abandonment: Giving up on one faith and/or leaving the Church
- Overwhelmed Apathy: So overwhelmed by the changes that one feels helpless, leading to apathy
- Denial: Turning away, working to deny these large scale cultural changes are real – or another form of denial is believing culture will return to what it was.
- Hyper-control: Creating more structure, rules, policies in an effort to control the change – rather than actually adjusting.
- Conflict: Remaining personally conflicted or engaging in conflict in the faith community due to these changes.

Cluster Two - Outdated Responses
Another set of common responses when change comes our way is to try what has worked before. This strategy is helpful when the models and paradigms we are using remain relevant, like during the Modern Era. These responses are more helpful than the reactions of Cluster One, yet they include limitations as well.

- Trying Harder: Doing the same activities and behaviors, yet with more vigor and effort.
- Spiritualizing: Believing the lack of adaptation is due to slack spirituality.
- Quality Improvement: Strengthening the quality of what you do in an effort to improve effectiveness.

Cluster Three - Proactive Adaptation
Letting go an outdated paradigm and moving into a time of adaptation is what actually facilitates healthy change.

- Letting Go: This is when/where individual disciples and churches realize the paradigm and model itself is no longer viable or relevant, developing the willingness to let it go.
- Purpose Seeking: When we let go of something, it drives us to foundational exploration. This response includes looking for the essential purpose of the Christian movement.
- Holy Experimenting: This response includes trying new behaviors, approaches and activities, not knowing what the outcome may be.
- Proactive Adaptation: Engaging the ongoing process of becoming a new disciple or new church who adapts to context regularly is proactive adaptation.

Where are you in your individual reaction or response?

Praying

What did you observe about you when it comes to responding to the changes in church life in these Postmodern times? Consider these insights in the context of dialogue with God.

Sending

Be who you are. You have no reason to apologize, nor hold back, when it comes to living out of your identity. God formed you and loves you. Now live like this is so.

Contexting – Day Six

Churches too. Churches also adapt and adjust to change. Look over the three clusters above, considering your faith community. Identify below which cluster you believe describes the essential position of your church at this point in its development. Include any notes in the blank space provided.

Cluster One - Defensive Reactions

Cluster Two - Outdated Responses

Cluster Three - Proactive Adaptation

Praying
You are invited to pray for your church today. Lift up your pastors, staff, lay leaders, and everyone else to God. Ask God to bless your church; helping each of you to be greater disciples and more fully join God's world transformation movement.

Sending
A journey of a thousand miles begins with the first step. You don't have to solve all the world's or the church's challenges today. All you are called to do is to take the next step. So, go forward today, taking the next step, trusting God will illumine the step after when it's time.

HARVESTING CONTEXTING

Gathering

As you gather, ask each person to share one change you have made in your life in the last month. This change can be minor to major, or anywhere in between. Then check in with each other...any news which anyone needs to share with the group?

Praying

Leader: We recognize, O God, that you were here before we arrived.

Group: We recognize, O God, that you are with us at all times, in all places.

Leader: Even before we made our way here, even before we moved through this day,

Group: You were here, waiting, anticipating our gathering in this place.

Leader: For you delight in your children, O God.

Group: When we gather in your name and in your Spirit, you rejoice.

Leader: So now, we also rejoice in you. We reflect on our lives this week and bring these items of gratitude to you, in the presence of these sisters and brothers in Christ:
(As you are moved, speak your gratitude aloud. As others share, silently lift their gratitude to God)

Leader: And now, O God, we also bring our concerns, as your children, to you as our loving heavenly parent:
(As you are moved, speak your concern aloud. As others share, silently lift their concerns to God)

Leader: And now, O God, we give you thanks for this opportunity to engage each other in life's pilgrimage.
Group: We ask that you fill us with your Holy Spirit and wrap this experience in your love.
All: Through the grace, power and love of Jesus Christ our Lord, may it be so. Amen.

Engaging
Major shifts are taking place in our larger world, as well as in our faith communities. Phyllis Tickle helps us understand these large-scale historical shifts in the Church. Now we are in the Transition Zone, moving from the Modern Era to the Postmodern Era. Individual Christians and/or particular local churches are unlikely to stop these large-scale cultural shifts, were we interested in doing so. Essentially, these shifts are not about our faith, they are about culture. Shifts in culture come and go. The role of faith is to strengthen and empower us to move through the shifts well.

Now let's consider how your church is relating to the shifting culture.
First, turn back to Daily Engagement Five from this past week.

The goal at this point in your discussion is simply to understand each point on the continuum, without identifying where your church may be.

Your Group Leader will more fully describe the nature of each point on this Developmental Response Continuum (Group Leaders: Include any insights from the Shift book to describe these as needed).

Second, the Group Leader will identify an imaginary straight line on the floor in the room where you are gathered. Group Leader will identify points for Cluster 1, 2, and 3 on this line. Now each disciple is invited to stand and go to the point on this imaginary line where you believe your church is in its response to these cultural shifts. After each person is standing, the Group Leader describes out loud what he/she sees. Then you are invited to return to your seat. The group leader invites people to describe why they stood where they did. Through this exploration your small group will gain perspective on your church's adaptive process.

Based on this activity, followed by debriefing your responses, what might this be saying about your church? What insights are here to gain?

Proactive Adaptation

Sometimes we human beings surprise ourselves. In actuality, we are very adaptable creatures. We are making changes in our lives all the time. Every day we learn new information, integrating it into the way we live. Were this not so, the human race would not have survived – or even more, thrived and proliferated as it has. So, we make changes all the time.

At the same time, we do not always bring this "change-friendly-perspective" to our church experience. A very common Christian belief is that God does not change; is the same yesterday, today and tomorrow. Given this, one can easily connect our church experience to our beliefs about God. Since God does not change, then God's Church remains exactly the same in its expression of itself. We don't consciously think this way, yet this perspective unconsciously guides decision-making in many churches.

Let's consider again Phyllis Tickle's description of the 500-year cycles in church history. One insight resulting from her work is that the church has changed many times over the course of our history. The church does have rummage sales. The church does adapt to its context when the context changes. This is not about changing the essence of our faith. This is about changing the way we live and express our faith. Evidently, God has guided our kind through major transitions many times through the centuries.

This is part of what it takes to move ourselves toward Proactive Adaptation; realizing that God can shepherd us through the changes necessary to adapt to our current context. So what about you?
What in your faith encourages you about the adaptability of your church? Not what is it about your church, but what is it in your understanding of God and God's ways which encourages you? What do you know from scripture, personal experience, tradition or the witness of others around you which gives you hope for your church as it journey's forward?
(Make time for discussion and sharing. Then the leader summarizes and brings this discussion to a close)

Previewing

This week you will engage the demise of member identity. The daily engagements will help you understand how the phrase "church member" has come to mean something which was not originally intended. Allow yourself to engage this learning, pondering and praying as you go.

Harvesting

Activity – Now consider your personal response to the large-scale shifts happening around us. Earlier you identified your church's response. Now how about you? Consider where you are in your development....then stand up and place yourself on the imaginary line at the fitting place. Remember, there is no shame no matter where you place yourself, so place yourself honestly. Do this activity in silence. While you are standing there, the Group Leader with share a Sending prayer with you.

Sending

O God, we are all works in progress. You call us to "work out our salvation with fear and trembling." We want to follow you into the present and future. We want to work out our salvation in ways which honor you and contribute life to this world. Help us now to take the next step. Help us now to continue our progression on this response continuum. Help us to embrace the challenges of our times, to be faithful spiritual pilgrims, on mission with you and each other. And now, to you be the glory, both now and forever more. Amen.

Daily Engagements
Member Identity

Member Identity – Day One

The word "member" is found 45 times in the New Testament. Only 8 of these references are in the gospels, with the remaining appearing in the pastoral epistles. Typically, member was used to describe our relationship to the church. Originally, the member metaphor was healthy and beautiful, describing an intricate relational body enjoying close connections.

Over time, the word member was co-opted by our larger culture, referring to the relationships among people in so many different kinds of organizations. Perhaps this story will help illustrate what I'm describing. While doing a Shift presentation in a retreat setting with leaders from a vibrant church, one of their staff members shared this story. A new family joined the church, bringing their young children. Neither parent was from a church background. After initially being very involved, this family withdrew from activities and worship participation. When someone contacted them, the wife described things this way: "We are having financial difficulties and we can't pay our membership dues right now (pledge). So, we don't want to use the services of the church when we can't pay our dues." This family was using what they know about membership in organizations from their culture to guide their church involvement.

Perhaps you can identify other ways in which the word "member" describes something other than what we mean when describing our relationship to God and each other as faith community participants. How has "church member" come to mean something organizational or institutional rather than spiritual?

_____

_____

_____

Praying

Being a part of the body of Christ is something of a mystery. How does God create these connections between us and God and each other? Consider asking God to heighten your conscious awareness about your identity as part of this great cloud of witnesses which make up the body of Christ.

Sending

Go today to the places where Christ went; to the hurting, dispossessed, infirm, looked-over, and left out. Be the hands and feet of Christ wherever you go.

Member Identity – Day Two

When it comes to describing who we are, "disciple" is the word most often used in the New Testament, appearing 263 times. Jesus uses this word in parables, stories, and teaching. We never describe those first committed followers of Jesus as the twelve church members. They were first disciples (followers) of Jesus Christ who connected with God and each other.

Now let's contrast the two sets of phrases below. Go ahead and read them out loud; allowing them to communicate their meaning to you.

I am a member of this church
I go to church
We are the members of this church

I am a disciple of Jesus Christ
I am the church
We are disciples of Jesus Christ who gather as this church

Given the challenging world in which we live, the descriptor "disciple" seems far more robust and substantive than the phrase "church member." Perhaps it's time to recover our disciple identities; learning to define ourselves first as disciples of Jesus Christ, rather than members of a certain local church. Our primary identity is disciple; disciples who join other disciples to form a local faith community.

Praying
How might embracing the identity of "disciple" change you? Invite God to shape you more into a disciple than a church

member (in the organizational sense).

Sending
We are disciples 24/7. We go to church (worship) a few hours each week. Go forward into your world today, knowing you are the church on the move.

Member Identity – Day Three

The following two word lists are like word association. They illustrate the differences which have evolved over time between church members and disciples.

Member Based Faith Community	Disciple Based Faith Community
Sacred or secular identity	Sacred identity
Transient	Permanence
Organizational focus	Relational focus
Institutional advancement	Health of the Body
Professionals provide services	Disciples serve each other
Settled	Sent

Who are you?

How has your faith journey taken shape over time? Reflecting on these two contrasting lists, identify which of these descriptors identify your perspective and identity. Try to lay aside which you prefer, instead identifying which actually describes where you are. Then, consider what this is telling you. How do you feel about what you are seeing?

_____

_____

_____

Praying

O God, I am a disciple because you have made me so.
In my life Lord, let it be. Amen.

Sending

As you go forth today may you lean into your salvation;

leaning into your identity as a baptized disciple of Jesus Christ.

Member Identity – Day Four

"I appreciate what we are talking about and am supportive of this movement. But I'm keenly aware that this language would scare people in our congregation. Our people are used to thinking of themselves as church members, but being disciples of Jesus Christ....that's a whole other way of thinking and relating which our church people aren't used to."

A lead pastor from a large, denominationally-based, numerically growing church made this statement as we were discussing this contrast between church member and disciple identity. I was thankful for this pastor's honesty in the context of a meeting with other pastors. At the same time, hearing this saddened me. When Christian people are resistant to being identified as disciples, then we have drifted a long way from our roots.

How do you feel about this whole disciple identity discussion? When you consider identifying yourself as a "disciple of Jesus Christ," what rises up in you? What presents itself to you as hesitation or resistance? For now, simply identify these.

_____

_____

_____

Praying

Look again at your response above. Invite God into your reflections now. What are you seeing in you as you engage this disciple identity discussion? In conversation with God, how might you pray today?

Sending

As you go about your way today, watch for God's kingdom rising up around you. When you see it, take note, and give glory to God.

Member Identity – Day Five

During the Modern Era, residents of North America were far more familiar with the stories of the Christian faith than now in this Postmodern Era. There was a general acceptance of the Christian faith in the larger culture. Many people were interested in church participation, believing this to be a helpful and healthy part of life.

Due to many shifts in our culture, Christianity is growing less favored in North America. Our faith is losing its majority status, finding itself less central to our culture. Given this, pilgrims in our communities who may come to faith in Jesus Christ do not follow the traditional patterns of faith development. In the past, inviting one to worship with you at your church was a common way to introduce someone to the Christian story. When there is a basic shared understanding and respect for the Christian story, then this is a helpful practice.

Now that fewer accept the Christian story as a legitimate way to understand ourselves and our world, engaging people with our faith is very different. Postmodern people have to experience something very real and substantive before they would consider believing the gospel. The gospel must be incarnated, taking on flesh and blood through demonstration, before Postmodern people believe its real. Attending a worship service may come toward the end of one's conversion process, rather than at the beginning.

What issues does this raise for you as a Christ-follower? For your faith community in the way it goes about being church?

_____

_____

_____

Praying
We as human beings are influenced by those around us. This is natural and normal. Ask God to help you receive influence from those who want good for you, rather than those who might guide you toward a "less-than" kind of existence.

Sending
No matter how culturally accepted your faith may be, this world is crying out for the love of God as expressed through Jesus Christ our Lord. Go today in the awareness that you are connected to the greatest transformational power this world has ever seen – God's love.

Member Identity – Day Six

Over the last 6 years, I have made a concerted effort to eliminate the phrase "church member" from my vocabulary. My motivation comes from all we have discussed in this week's Daily Engagements. Jesus never used the phrase "church member(s)" in the gospels. Jesus described his followers as "disciples." As I continue onward in this journey, seeing myself less as a church member and more as a disciple, I notice changes in my faith. It's growing more personal, more present throughout each week, and more vitalized.

Were you to engage this same word experiment; referring to yourself and others as disciple(s) and not church members….how might this influence you? What shifts might you notice in yourself and in your pilgrimage through this world?

_____

_____

_____

Praying
You are invited to consider praying that God will help you lay aside any hesitation about accepting your identity as a disciple of Jesus Christ.

Sending
Go now in the awareness that you ARE one of God's people. You ARE the church. You ARE sufficient to the calling which lays before you this very day.

HARVESTING MEMBER IDENTITY

Gathering

Roles. We all live out of multiple roles all the time.
Collectively name some of your roles, like son, employee,
owner, Rotary Club member, plumber, etc. Then, consider
which of these roles means the most to you these days. Do a
go around, giving the opportunity to identify your answer
with a brief explanation why this role is valuable to you now.
-Also, check to see if there is any news disciples need to share
(positive, negative, neutral) which this group may want/need
to know.

Praying

Leader: We recognize, O God, that you were here before we
arrived.

Group: We recognize, O God, that you are with us at all times,
in all places.

Leader: Even before we made our way here, even before we
moved through this day,

Group: You were here, waiting, anticipating our gathering in
this place.

Leader: For you delight in your children, O God.

Group: When we gather in your name and in your Spirit, you rejoice.

Leader: So now, we also rejoice in you. We reflect on our lives this week and bring these items of gratitude to you, in the presence of these sisters and brothers in Christ:

(As you are moved, speak your gratitude aloud. As others share, silently lift their gratitude to God)

Leader: And now, O God, we also bring our concerns, as your children, to you as our loving heavenly parent:

(As you are moved, speak your concern aloud. As others share, silently lift their concerns to God)

Leader: And now, O God, we give you thanks for this opportunity to engage each other in life's pilgrimage.

Group: We ask that you fill us with your Holy Spirit and wrap this experience in your love.

All: Through the grace, power and love of Jesus Christ our Lord, may it be so. Amen.

Engaging

Early in our discussion about shifting from member identity to disciple identity, we may think we are making a mountain out of a molehill. What does it really matter what we call ourselves? Isn't it all just semantics?

Perhaps an illustrations will help.

When people start running for exercise, they will sometimes self-identify as "joggers." This word is not used as much as it once was, yet we often hear people denying they are runners. When they are beginners, or hesitant about their abilities, they will often say things like, "I'm not a runner; I go running." Or others will say, "I'm a jogger, but hope to become a runner as I improve." Instinctively people know that describing oneself as a runner means something. The labels we use for ourselves communicate to us and others how we perceive ourselves.

Day Three Engagement this week contrasted member and disciple. Engage this discussion in your group. *First,* when you describe yourselves as church members, what does that mean to you? What associations rise up for you? Discuss together what this might mean about this self-description. *Second*, when you describe yourselves as disciples, what does that mean to you? What associations rise up for you? How does this shift your faith journey? Were you to embrace this self-description more fully, what would it mean for your faith journey?

Postmodern pilgrims don't carry much regard for positional authority; giving authority to those who earn their trust. When it comes to believing the faith story of a religion, again they must observe that faith in action in order to trust its reliability. Just because one says it is so is not convincing when people do not have trustworthy people in their lives giving witness to this faith story.

One outcome of this shift in our culture is that the bar for Christ-like living is raised. In order to be witnesses of our faith, we must live it, authentically. There is no room for tepid faith expression. For postmodern people to believe what we say about our faith, they must see it demonstrated in real life. So what does this mean for we Christ-following pilgrims? What does this mean for our churches?

First, discuss how we would know when we are living our faith. What kind of people would we be and what actions would we take?

_____

_____

_____

Second, how could we help each other to actually live this way? If we are sacred partners on this journey, how can we contribute to each other, helping us live in the Way of Jesus Christ?

_____

_____

_____

Previewing
Living as disciples of Jesus Christ....
God's Church is uniquely tasked with the commission to make disciples. So how do we do this? This week's Daily Engagements lead us into consideration of what forms us as disciples.

Harvesting
Do a go around, giving disciples the opportunity to fill in the blank:

Were I to lay aside member identity, embracing more fully my identity as a disciple of Jesus Christ, this would influence me to _____.

Sending

(Read responsively, with heart!)

Leader: Now, as we go, we go in the awareness that we ARE God's people.

Group: God's creative Spirit brought us into this world.

Leader: God's power sustains us to this very moment.

Group: So let's go, embracing who we are in Christ.

Leader: Let's go as salt, to flavor this world.

Group: Let's go as light, to shine in the darkness.

Leader: Let's go as grace, to bring healing and hope to this broken and hurting world.

All: And may the peace of God, which surpasses all comprehension, guard our hearts and minds in Christ Jesus until we meet again. Amen.

Daily Engagements
Disciple Identity

Disciple Identity – Day One

"The writers and printers of this book take no responsibility for the actions of readers after exposure to the images, concepts, people, and teachings contained herein. All claims due to discomfort and lifestyle disruption will be denied, while all stories of abundant life, deeper meaning, and wild abandon with grace will be celebrated. No discounts or special offers apply – all readers are equally in danger. Reader discretion is advised. Proceed at your own risk."

Disclaimer which should
be on the cover of
every New Testament

"Do not look for shortcuts to God. The market is flooded with surefire, easygoing formulas for a successful life that can be practiced in your spare time. Do not fall for that stuff, even though crowds of people do. The way to life – to God! – is vigorous and requires total attention."

Jesus, Matthew 7:13-14
The Message

So what does it mean to live in the Way of Jesus? How would our lives change if we lived by the Sermon on the Mount found in Matthew or the Sermon on the Plain found in Luke? After reading the warning above from Matthew 7, I found myself thinking there ought to be a warning statement plastered on every Bible. That last phrase in Matthew 7…"*is vigorous and requires total attention,*" is haunting. These kinds of statements make it very clear that living in the Way of Jesus is a way of life, rather than simply being a nice, considerate person (though it may include that at times). Though it will cost us everything (buying the field with the treasure beyond price therein), we will discover life beyond measure.

Praying

How ready are you? How ready are you to engage the scriptures and other disciples around living as a disciple? Consider asking God to remove from your life anything which interferes with your disciple development.

Sending

As you go today, give yourself to God. Go with your face set toward living into your calling with enthusiasm, commitment, and vigor. Live this day as if you wanted to make the most of every opportunity to be alive.

Disciple Identity – Day Two

"A rule of life is a pattern of spiritual disciplines that
provide structure and direction for growth in
holiness. When we speak of patterns in our if, we
mean attitudes, behaviors, or elements that are
routine, repeated, regular. ..A rule of life is not mean
to be restrictive, although it asks for genuine
commitment. .....It fosters gifts of the Spirit in
personal life and human community, helping to form
us into the persons God intends us to be."

Marjorie Thompson
Soulfeast: An Invitation To The
Christian Spiritual Life, 1995

How do we grow in our disciple identities? How can we help
ourselves and one another move along the disciple pathway?
During the Middle Ages, the monastics tended to gather
themselves into communities which were centered in a "Rule
of Life." These were practices they believed would contribute
to their formation and expression as disciples. Now, in these
Postmodern times, Christ-followers are rediscovering the
practice of a Rule of Life (ROL). Some congregations are
engaging in discernment around what practices they believe
could be an effective ROL for them. They begin with the
question, "What practices do we believe could form us
disciples?"

Before we give you examples, go ahead and consider what a
personal ROL might be. Recall times when you were really
growing as a disciple, along with what you were doing which
contributed to that growth. As you observe your own spiritual

journey, you will begin identifying your ROL.

_____

_____

_____

Praying

Who are those disciples who have loved you, shaped you, and helped you move ahead in your spiritual journey? Pause and give thanks for at least 3 people right now.

Sending

You too can be a person who makes someone else's list. You can influence others toward what is good, pure, and life giving. As you go today, look for the opportunities to use your influence to help others grow in their faith.

Disciple Identity – Day Three

The following are ROL examples. They range from general to specific. Use them to help yourself consider what your personal ROL may be.

1. Service
2. Simplicity
3. Creativity
4. Obedience
5. Prayer
6. Community
7. Love

Seven (Christian Community)
San Francisco, Soul Graffiti
Mark Scandrette, 2007

1. Pray daily
2. Worship weekly
3. Read the Bible
4. Serve at and beyond Prince of Peace
5. Be in relationship to encourage spiritual growth in others
6. Give of my time, talent, and resource

Michael Foss
Six Marks of Discipleship
For A Changing Church, 2000

- Worshipping God weekly
- Praying and reading scripture daily
- Engaging in a Christian formation-focused small group
- Giving generously of my time, talent, and treasure
- Sharing my faith story with those ready to hear
- Serving vigorously, making a difference in the world

Church, who during their
visioning process, decided
they needed a ROL

Now, what about you? Record your insights about what spiritual disciplines or practices may contribute to your formation as a disciple of Jesus Christ.

_____

_____

_____

Praying
Remember at least one holy moment you shared with God at some point during this life's pilgrimage. Recognize that holy moment as a gift from God. Express your thanks to God.

Sending
As you go, live in the afterglow of that remembered holy moment. Reconnect with the spiritual energy which resulted from that experience and live out of that deep well today.

Disciple Identity – Day Four

Christian formation is best done in the context of Christian relationships. We human beings are social beings, discovering our identities in the context of community (family, friends, church, etc.). Each ROL sample from yesterday includes being in relationship with others for disciple development purposes. So it turns out that Christian formation focused small groups are an excellent way to help one another live out a ROL.

Most churches practice some form of small groups, while not all small groups are created equal. Some of these are more focused on forming people into disciples than others. What about the small group(s) in which you are involved? How much do these small groups contribute to your development as a disciple? Would you recommend this form of disciple development to someone else who really wants to pursue discipleship? What might need changing for your small group to grow more purposeful in its disciple development?

_____
_____
_____

Praying
If you do not have a disciple developing-focused small group, pray for one now.
If you are in a disciple developing small group, give thanks for it now.

Sending
Sometimes others perceive us as better persons than we perceive ourselves to be. Identify one positive quality or

characteristic which others see in you, but which you doubt. Go forth today, living like their perception of you is real and authentic.

Disciple Identity – Day Five

Who is interested in your formation as a disciple?
No really – Who cares enough about you to inquire about
your disciple development?
For many of us, we are rarely in relationship with someone
wherein our discipleship growth is part of our typical
conversations. Oddly enough, even in churches people are
sometimes reluctant to engage serious conversations about
their own faith journeys.

Discussion: What's this about? What contributes to our
hesitancy when it comes to sharing our faith journeys with
each other? Given this (hesitancies), what do we need in
order to grow more at ease around sharing; talking with each
other about our faith? How might you integrate this into your
church experience?

_____

_____

_____

Praying
Dare we pray that we will be more bold in sharing our faith
with each other? Consider asking God to help you speak very
naturally about your faith journey when the time is right.

Sending
As you go today, watch for the opportunity to share
something from your faith journey which may be encouraging
and helpful to someone.

Disciple Identity – Day Six

Christian Education to Christian Formation to Disciple Development....

These phrases represent our evolving understanding when it comes to being formed as disciples. In the 20th century, we described the process as Christian Education. This presupposes that gaining knowledge through education forms us as disciples. Gaining knowledge, learning the Christian story, is a necessary part of our journeys. On the other hand, we recognize now that knowledge alone rarely leads to transformation. Later churches began using the phrase Christian Formation, making progress toward a more accurate description of what we are about. Now we are recommending that churches update their language again, using the phrase Disciple Development to describe our growth process.

You are invited to try these on for fit. Say each of the three phrases at the beginning of the previous paragraph out loud....slowly. Which is more attractive to you? Which draws you forward?

Praying
You are invited to embrace the process of Disciple Development today. Consider asking God to develop you further as a disciple this very day. Inquire of God what you might do to contribute to this process.

Sending

As you go, know that you are a disciple.

As you go, know that you are becoming a disciple.

As you go, know that God will complete your growth process as a disciple at the end of all things.

As you go, rejoice!

HARVESTING DISCIPLE IDENTITY

Gathering

On Youtube.com, show the group "How He Loves" by John Mark McMillan. The pictures are designed by Si Smith.
https://www.youtube.com/watch?v=O5bfxGNMY9c
Watch in silence, allowing this experience to engage you. When this music ends, allow a few moments of silence, and then draw this time to a close.

Share any updates or news you want your Small Group to know.

Praying

Leader: We recognize, O God, that you were here before we arrived.

Group: We recognize, O God, that you are with us at all times, in all places.

Leader: Even before we made our way here, even before we moved through this day,

Group: You were here, waiting, anticipating our gathering in this place.

Leader: For you delight in your children, O God.

Group: When we gather in your name and in your Spirit, you rejoice.

Leader: So now, we also rejoice in you. We reflect on our lives this week and bring these items of gratitude to you, in the presence of these sisters and brothers in Christ:

(As you are moved, speak your gratitude aloud. As others share, silently lift their gratitude to God)

Leader: And now, O God, we also bring our concerns, as your children, to you as our loving heavenly parent:

(As you are moved, speak your concern aloud. As others share, silently lift their concerns to God)

Leader: And now, O God, we give you thanks for this opportunity to engage each other in life's pilgrimage.

Group: We ask that you fill us with your Holy Spirit and wrap this experience in your love.

All: Through the grace, power and love of Jesus Christ our Lord, may it be so. Amen.

Engaging

The Day One Engagement this week included a potential disclaimer statement for the preface of the Bible. The challenges of living as an authentic disciple are heightened in this Day One Engagement. The author seems to believe that living in the Way of Jesus will disrupt our lifestyles, shaking us up.

Discussion: What do you think? How so? Is this a new kind of legalism or rules-oriented kind of faith? If not, to what might the author be referring?

Rule of Life

This week we engaged the ROL concept. These are not "rules for life," but instead are spiritual practices which can contribute to our development as disciples. The monastics gathered their community around their practices, using these to develop one another as disciples. The New Monastics, emerging faith communities, as well as traditional denominationally based churches are doing the same.

This is an opportunity for you and your Small Group to consider what your ROL might be. Several times this week you were invited to reflect on spiritual practices which have been formational for you. Also, you considered what might become the ROL for your church.

Activity

1. The Group Leader will facilitate rotation around your circle wherein each disciple identifies one spiritual practice with is formative. The Group Leader will record these (white board, flip chart, or some other way in which all can see them – if you are able). If someone ahead of you mentions the same one you are intending to mention, then go to your next choice. After going around the circle you will have a list of meaningful ROL practices.

2. Next, consider your church as a whole. Looking at this list and knowing your church as you do, collectively identify ROL practices which you believe your church could embrace and integrate. You can include those on the previous list which you prefer, while also creating new practices which are not yet

mentioned. After identifying, narrow your list to 7 or less (more is overwhelming).

3. When your list is complete with 7 or less ROL practices, step back and reflect on them. Ask yourselves how much you believe these practices would form your faith community as Christian disciples. When finished, the Group Leader will share this list with the point person in your church identified to receive them.

Discussion: Now, you don't have to wait for the church to decide on its collective ROL to begin. If you wanted to begin this week, which of these might you choose to implement? How ready are you to do so?

Previewing
This coming week's Daily Engagements introduce us to the Attractional Church. This phrase describes a primary dynamic around which churches formed themselves during the Modern Era. You will very likely recognize your church in the Attractional Church description. Decide now to adopt a learner's attitude, preparing yourself to engage well, laying defensiveness or resistance aside. Trust this will facilitate a good learning experience for you this week.

Harvesting
We have covered much ground this Small Group. What are you gaining from this experience?
Do a go around, inviting each person to share one insight.

Sending

Leader: Fruits of the Spirit are love, joy, peace, patience, kindness, goodness, faithfulness, gentleness, and self-control. Our lives are God's vineyard, where this fruit is grown. Our world is hungry for the savory flavors of this holy fruit. May you go forth, flowering and blossoming, as God's good work ripens in your life this very week.

Group: So be it!

All: Amen!

Daily Engagements
Attractional Church

Attractional Church – Day One

Alan Roxburgh has written extensively on the Attractional Church, saying that 90% of North American churches are attractional in nature. "Attractional" describes the tendency of churches to focus on attracting people to what they are doing in an effort to gain more members. In fact, according to Roxburgh, this is the primary assumption of the Attractional Church: *People are looking for a church, either consciously or unconsciously. Therefore, our goal is to become as attractive as possible.*

When we reflect on our activities as churches, we realize that nearly all our activities are built upon this assumption; one that held truth in it in the Modern Era. Now that we are in Postmodern times, the pool of people who are looking for a church because they accept the basic premises of Christianity, is smaller every day. So what about your context? How much has it changed from the Modern Era? Are people still looking for a church, even though they may not be involved in one? What insights come to you as you consider the church described as attractional?

_____

_____

_____

Praying

Authentic and genuine faith expression is needed in our world, a movement based on love. This is what Jesus came to this world to do, to initiate a better way. Consider praying that you will live in ways which advance this movement of love today.

Sending

As you go, watch for the opportunity to love others who need loved. Trust that God will give you a compassionate spirit toward those you are called to love today.

Attractional Church – Day Two

There was a time in North America (1950s-1980s) when churches who provided two or three quality ministries were thriving; numerically speaking. The Modern Era culture remained intact, with churches enjoying their majority culture privileges. Now, churches can provide the same programs and ministries with high quality, but with smaller return on investment (ROI). There is nothing wrong with what these churches are doing, providing excellent programming. It's just that the culture which supported that way of being church shifted. Now these churches experience a lower return on their investment in programming when it comes to attracting people to what they are doing.

Consider the people you know who are not Christ-followers. How much do they seem to be consciously or unconsciously looking for a church? How much is church part of their value system – or even on their radar screens? And, if finding a church to attend is not a priority for them, what questions does that raise for how your church does church?

_____

_____

_____

Praying
Jesus described the kingdom as being among us. Consider praying for the eyes to see and ears to hear the kingdom's appearing today.

Sending
Who do you know who is not a Christ-follower, but who has great passion for improving your community? As you go,

consider asking this person what motivates him/her in his/her efforts to make this world better. Practice respectful listening as you inquire. Thank him/her for sharing.

Attractional Church – Day Three

The demise of the Attractional Church raises many questions for Postmodern disciples. The most foundational question is, "So what's the purpose of this Christian Movement anyway?" During the Modern Era, clergy and church staff developed short-hand ways for describing how we measure progress as churches. The Three Bs is one of those ways: Buildings, Bodies, and Budgets. First we wanted to build more buildings, or at least maintain those we had. Second, we wanted to add more people (bodies) to our membership lists. Third, we wanted to increase, or at least maintain, our financial budgets. When we were progressing in these three ways, then we were generally considered to be a successful church. Denominations tended to adopt this perspective, integrating the Three Bs into the reporting forms completed annually by each church.

But now the scorecard, so to speak, is different. The ROI on our programmatic and ministry work is lower due to large-scale cultural shifts. Most churches cannot expect the same results from their efforts at attracting people to what they are doing. As we have already discussed, there are many ways churches are responding to this shifting dynamic (Developmental Response Continuum). The best response is to allow the crisis this culture shift creates to drive us back to one foundational question: What's the purpose of The Church anyway?

Praying
Consider praying for wisdom to discern God's calling for your church. You might focus your prayer to simply the next step forward as a church.

Sending

Jesus gave a New Commandment, that we love one another like he loves us. By this others will know we are disciples. Go forward today, trusting that God has empowered you to love others because God has made you God's own.

Attractional Church – Day Four

"If you build it, they will come."
Remember this statement from the 1989 film Field Of Dreams, starring Kevin Costner? This is the perfect motto for the Attractional Church.

Here is the challenge for those of us who have been a part of the Christian Movement for some time: we are so immersed in the Attractional perspective that we feel confused and disoriented, or even like we are betraying something sacred, when we question the Attractional Model. But we have to ask ourselves what Jesus modeled for us when it comes to inviting people to church....

Nothing.
Jesus never invited anyone to church.
(Pause for a moment, allowing this insight to sink into your awareness)
Instead, Jesus went to people, engaging them where they were, mingling freely with the people of the land.

Praying
Who are the people, or even just one person, who needs your interest, attention, and love today? If you can identify him/her/them, pray now that you will love them as God calls you today. If you don't know who needs you in this way, consider praying that God will show you as you go along today.

Sending
Ask God to confirm your praying (above) and then set your sights on living with love today.

Attractional Church – Day Five

In the Shift book, the author describes a large church which is extreme in its efforts to be attractional. This church advertised that it would give away a Jeep Grand Cherokee to one lucky worshipper on a particular Sunday. During the weeks before the big giveaway day, they publicized this event throughout their city. Sure enough, on the designated Sunday, one worshipper was given the keys to this beautiful new SUV. Evidently, this church believes that attracting people to what we are doing is worth extreme measures.

As previously noted, author Alan Roxburgh says that 90% of North American churches are attractional. This likely includes your church. So, begin considering the alternative to being attractional. If getting people to church activities is not the primary purpose of the church, then what are we about?

_____

_____

_____

Praying
Holy imagination...this is what it takes to dream dreams and see new visions. Consider praying for God to stir your imagination about what church could be.

Sending
The Holy Spirit shows up in scripture as fire, wind, and even a dove. As you go today, know that this Spirit lives in you, because you are God's own. Listen for the Spirit's guidance as you go through your day.

Attractional Church – Day Six

Clarification: We are not suggesting that churches intentionally become unattractive in who they are and what they do. Anytime we do anything as churches, we aspire to excellence and quality. Whatever our hands find to do, we are called to do it as if it's for God.

So being an attractional church is not wrong or bad, it simply is not the primary focus of the gospel. Of course we don't believe that the Christian movement's goal is to get big numbers to events. Is this what the incarnation of Jesus Christ was about – to get people to our churches? No, the incarnation of Jesus Christ was about bringing the kingdom of God to earth, establishing it, and helping it to flourish. We are about God's kingdom coming on earth, as it is in heaven.

Jesus was willing to lay down his life for this kingdom's progress. To the best of our ability to discern, how much does the way we "do church" reflect the purpose, values and teachings of Jesus Christ?

Praying
Today, you are invited to pray for your church as it moves along the Developmental Response Continuum. Consider praying that your church will jump two places ahead as a result of engaging this Making The Shift Experience.

Sending
God is making us into new creations, every day. As you go today, look for how you are changing, more clearly reflecting your Savior and Lord, Jesus Christ.

HARVESTING ATTRACTIONAL CHURCH

Gathering

During this life's journey, we come to times of significant transition. Reflect on your journey thus far, identifying a particular challenging transition for you. What was it like? How did it challenge you? Ultimately, what was it that helped you move through that transition?

(Break into pairs so that each person has opportunity to describe their transition to a partner. Remember, this is a no shame group, so you are not required to share out loud.)

-Share any updates or news you want your Small Group to know.

Praying

Leader: We recognize, O God, that you were here before we arrived.

Group: We recognize, O God, that you are with us at all times, in all places.

Leader: Even before we made our way here, even before we

moved through this day,

Group: You were here, waiting, anticipating our gathering in this place.

Leader: For you delight in your children, O God.

Group: When we gather in your name and in your Spirit, you rejoice.

Leader: So now, we also rejoice in you. We reflect on our lives this week and bring these items of gratitude to you, in the presence of these sisters and brothers in Christ:

(As you are moved, speak your gratitude aloud. As others share, silently lift their gratitude to God)

Leader: And now, O God, we also bring our concerns, as your children, to you as our loving heavenly parent:

(As you are moved, speak your concern aloud. As others share, silently lift their concerns to God)

Leader: And now, O God, we give you thanks for this opportunity to engage each other in life's pilgrimage.

Group: We ask that you fill us with your Holy Spirit and wrap this experience in your love.

All: Through the grace, power and love of Jesus Christ our Lord, may it be so. Amen.

Engaging

This week's Daily Engagements focused on deconstructing the Attractional Church paradigm. Engaging this process can be difficult and even painful. This can feel like loss, involving grief. In addition, sincere questions rise for us when we deconstruct a cherished model for how to be church, like these below:

"Does God not care about the church anymore?"

"Are our buildings going to become museums, like what happened in Europe?"

"Why isn't God blessing our efforts anymore?"

"This used to work (events, program, quality services). Why isn't it working now (drawing crowds)?"

"Wouldn't we reach more people if we just _____ (fill in the blank with myriads of ideas)?"

So now we are in a state of crisis due to what we see happening around us. This crisis is theological, with people questioning their faith and belief systems. This crisis is methodological, as churches are realizing their paradigm no longer resonates to its former degree with their ministry context. I'm sure there are additional crisis beyond these very obvious ones we have named. Where does this leave God's people and God's church? (Discuss how you are feeling and what you are thinking in light of this process)

Perhaps this is a good time to remember the words of Scripture.

Throughout the Bible, the writers frequently address fear. "Do not be afraid," is a directive appearing so many times in the Bible that it's certainly a major theme. God, angels, prophets and very ordinary people verbalize this directive over and over. So on the one hand, we may experience emotions and thinking related to loss and fear. At the same time, we move on to our faith, remembering who we follow and who we can trust in times of transition.

As a group consider the two columns below and identify your responses. This is a way to process what is happening for you in the moment, facilitating movement and progress. Honesty at this point is very helpful, realizing many of us are a mixture of both columns.

(Leaders – give a few minutes for disciples to make notes, then discuss)

Fear and Loss-Based Feelings and Thoughts	Faith and Trust-Based Feelings and Thoughts

Now look over your list in the Faith and Trust column above. What stands out for you? What may be God's word for you now? What else do you need to discuss with this group which may free you to move onward toward Proactive Adaptation?

Previewing
> "...we have begun to learn that the Biblical message
> is more radical, more inclusive, and more
> transforming than we allowed it to be. In particular,
> we have begun to see that the church of Jesus Christ
> is not the purpose or goal of the gospel, but rather
> its instrument."

> Darrell Guder,
> *Missional Church: A Vision For The*

Sending Of The Church In North America

What now?

Joining God on mission in the world. That is the calling of the Missional Church. This week we will engage God's call to participate with God in the unveiling of God's kingdom.

Harvesting

"When the going gets tough, the tough get going."
(Dated and worn-out folk wisdom)
As you move ahead in your spiritual pilgrimage, what from this Small Group gathering will you take with you which gives you "strength of soul" (Psalm 138 phrase)?
(Do a go around)

Sending

Leader: Soul of Christ, sanctify me; body of Christ, save me; blood of Christ, inebriate me;

Group: water from the side of Christ, wash me; passion of Christ, strengthen me.

Leader: O good Jesus, hear me; within your wounds hide me; suffer me not to be separated from you;

Group: from the malicious enemy defend me; in the hour of my death call me; and bid me come to you

All: that with your saints I may praise you forever and ever. Amen

Midday Prayer, Common Prayer
A Liturgy For Ordinary Radicals

Daily Engagements
Missional Church

Missional Church – Day One

"Missio Dei" = The Mission of God
Before we launch too far into this Missional Church
Movement discussion, let's start with basics. Is the goal for
we Christ-followers to establish God's Church? Or, is our goal
to join God's mission in the world?
Consider the following cartoon from Karl Barth For Dummies
on Facebook.

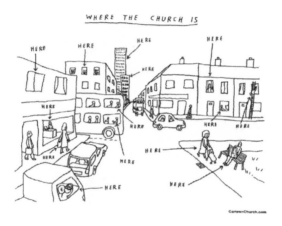

What meaning do you interpret from this sketch? What kind
of contrasts are here regarding the Attractional Church
paradigm? What would happen if your faith community
embraced the meaning of this sketch at higher levels?

_____

_____

_____

Praying
God's kingdom involves reconciliation, healing, and
restoration. Consider who you know who may need one of

these. Will you pray that God's kingdom will come today in the life of that person?

Sending
Sometimes disciples are described as the hand and feet of Christ. As you go today, do something to contribute to reconciliation, healing, or restoration.

Missional Church – Day Two

Here is another sketch; this one by David Hayward of nakedpreacher.com. Slow down and look at this sketch. Allow your mind to go where it will, noting your insights. Record them below this sketch.

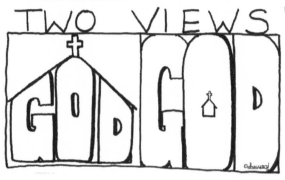

_____

_____

_____

From the vantage point of most of us North American Christ-followers, we are used to viewing the world from the first block, an attractional church understanding of God's ways. God is found at church. Then the church does missions. Therefore the church has a mission to accomplish. The second block gives us a visual of the missional church perspective. God is expansive. God preceded the church. God continues the mission God began long before the church was born. The church is an instrument of God's activity for bringing God's reign on earth. The kingdom of God is here and is also coming. The church is one example of the kingdom. Therefore God has a mission to accomplish, and the church is called to join God in that mission.

The following statement would make a great caption for David Hayward's illustration above.

> "It is not the church of God that has a mission, it is the God of mission that has a church."
> *Rowan Williams, (Former) Archbishop of Canterbury*

Praying
What draws you into God's mission? Where is your place to serve? Consider asking God for clarity on our role in the kingdom today.

Sending
Go now, knowing you are salt, light, and grace. This world needs disciples like you, determined to be who God believes you to be.

Missional Church – Day Three

Primary Assumption of the Missional Church – God is on mission in the world, unveiling the kingdom, while reconciling and healing the world.

Let's put these insights from this week together. First, God is on mission in the world. The Church is present in the world 24/7, as disciples go about their lives. Second, God was on mission before the Church existed. God is larger than the Church. Third, God is active in the world, unveiling the kingdom while reconciling and healing the world.

When we view God and the Church through this Missional lens, we come the following striking insights:

1. God's mission is not to save your church
2. The degree to which your church joins God on mission is the degree to which your church will be saved
3. Your church's salvation is in giving itself away (not in protecting itself or focusing on survival)

Capture your reactions to these three statements below. Also, consider what this might mean for how your faith community is church.

_____

_____

_____

Praying
We are exploring foundational and critical concepts about the nature of God and God's Church. Consider what is rising up in

you as you engage this process. Consider lifting your thought and feelings to God right now. "Cast your cares on him, for he cares for you."

Sending

Yes, we are called to love others. This means there are those in your world who are called to love you. How open are you to being loved, receiving grace, and allowing yourself to be the recipient of God's love through other disciples? Go today, opening yourself to receive.

Missional Church – Day Four

"This is a time for a dramatically new vision. The current predicament of churches in North America requires more than mere tinkering with long-assumed notions about identity and mission of the church. Instead, as many knowledgeable observers have noted, there is a need for reinventing or rediscovering the church in this new kind of world."

George Hunsberger in Missional Church

For those of us who have been a part of this Christian Movement for some time, shifting our perspective from Attractional to Missional is no small endeavor. This is a shift of monumental proportions. The following three insights are designed to help us let go of our attachment to the Attractional Church paradigm and ready ourselves to join God on mission.

1. *We must accept that church- as-we-have-known-it is not returning, letting go of our expectations that it will return, along with our actions designed to bring it back*
2. *We must accept our context for what it is, letting go of anger or bitterness directed toward our society and culture*
3. *We must accept the church is facing adaptive challenges just like all other organizations and institutions in our society, releasing the desire to enshrine one way of being church*

We provide these three clear statements due to the complexity and strength of our attachment to the

Attractional Church Model. What do you find rising up in you as you consider them?

_____

_____

_____

Praying

Confession sometimes refers to releasing sin to God. Other times confession is describing our vulnerabilities and pain to God. Consider engaging confession with God, focusing on whatever is important to you now.

Sending

God's grace is sufficient for us. The Apostle Paul experienced God's graceful provision, even when he felt broken and vulnerable. Go in the awareness that God's grace is sufficient for you this very day.

Missional Church – Day Five

What then? Once we let go of the Attractional Model and embrace our Missional calling, what's our next step? This is when we are ready for Holy Experimenting.

First we engage our context, our community, with open and receptive ears, eyes, hearts, and minds. We hope to learn where God is active in this community. We want to meet people, learn from them, and strengthen relationships and connections. We are eager to recognize assets and strengths, as well as seeing the brokenness. Then we take this learning to the gospel. We ask what the good news of Christ has to do with what we learn in and from our community. Where do the gospel and what we see in our community align? Then we move to considering what we might do as a congregation. This is when we engage in holy experimenting. When we are holy experimenting,

- We engage in activities without knowing the outcome beforehand
- We are making our best guesses about what might contribute to God's kingdom
- We recognize and accept that experiments may lead to any number of outcomes, each a step forward
- We continue our "learner's attitude," staying open to God's intervention as we go along
- We discover unforeseen new missional pathways, given our experimentation orientation
- We are able to pivot quickly, updating our action-plan as we move along

- We give ourselves freedom to try many new missional engagement actions without over-burdening them with expectations of "success"

I'm reading an excellent book filled with spiritual guidance by Brian McLaren, *We Make The Road By Walking*. The book title is not original, often used to describe life's journey. McLaren makes the case for discovering a new way of life by moving ahead; by standing up and moving forward in trust and faith. God's guidance often occurs as we are moving forward, rather than before our first steps. This is what holy experimenting is about. We learn from our community, we engage the gospel, and then launch out into missional engagement. Course corrections will happen as we move forward. We will encounter dead end streets, having to back up and make another turn. We will find beautiful vistas which expand our spirits and enliven our hearts. We will discover what life in the kingdom of God is about. Holy experimenting is a perspective and attitude which allows us to make the road by walking.

Praying
When the Son has set you free, you are free indeed. Give thanks to God for your freedom to live as God created and designed you, with no hesitation nor apology.

Sending
How about experimenting today? Do something today which is out of the ordinary for you. Allow curiosity and learning to be your guide, not a desire for perfection or performance, as you experiment.

Missional Church – Day Six

After engaging in Missional activity, bring your stories back to your faith community.

Though the word testimonies fell from grace in our common language, story-telling still resonates with us as a powerful way to express our faith journeys. Your missional engagement strategy needs a communication feedback loop. After engaging the community with an eye toward learning and connection, then you are ready to share what you are learning and experiencing. This is a great time for disciples to address the larger church, typically during worship. Some may choose other forms of communication, like newsletters, email blasts, social media, etc. The point is that sharing our missional engagement stories energizes those who hear. We vicariously experience missional engagement, warming our hearts and encouraging our doing. We are far more likely to join the missional movement when we hear another disciple telling his/her story than when we only hear missional engagement described. Look for every opportunity to tell stories about how your intention is happening, how missional engagement is taking shape.

Even now, consider a missional engagement story from your experience. Consider sharing it in your next Small Group gathering.

Praying
Consider asking God's guidance in choosing a missional engagement story from your experience. If you cannot identify any, then consider asking God to guide you to missional engagement today.

Sending

There is no time like the present. Follow the energy today. Follow the Spirit's lead into caring actions with someone somewhere during your day today.

SMALL GROUP SEVEN
HARVESTING MISSIONAL CHURCH

Gathering

We are at week seven now. Given the nature and activities of this group, you are getting to know one another. To help you connect even further, do a go around wherein you share something you are learning about or from the person to your left. Make sure each person is included in this gathering activity.

Share any updates or news you want this Small Group to know.

Praying

Leader: We recognize, O God, that you were here before we arrived.

Group: We recognize, O God, that you are with us at all times, in all places.

Leader: Even before we made our way here, even before we moved through this day,

Group: You were here, waiting, anticipating our gathering in this place.

131

Leader: For you delight in your children, O God.

Group: When we gather in your name and in your Spirit, you rejoice.

Leader: So now, we also rejoice in you. We reflect on our lives this week and bring these items of gratitude to you, in the presence of these sisters and brothers in Christ:

(As you are moved, speak your gratitude aloud. As others share, silently lift their gratitude to God)

Leader: And now, O God, we also bring our concerns, as your children, to you as our loving heavenly parent:

(As you are moved, speak your concern aloud. As others share, silently lift their concerns to God)

Leader: And now, O God, we give you thanks for this opportunity to engage each other in life's pilgrimage.

Group: We ask that you fill us with your Holy Spirit and wrap this experience in your love.

All: Through the grace, power and love of Jesus Christ our Lord, may it be so. Amen.

Engaging

Part One

Look again at the sketch from Day Two this week: Two Views Of God. Engage one another in discussion regarding your reactions to this sketch. What did you write on the reaction lines for Day Two? During this week, where has your thinking gone in relation to this sketch? (Group Discussion)

"It is not the church of God that has a mission, it is the God of mission that has a church."
Rowan Williams, Archbishop of Canterbury

132

Part Two

Where is the center of God's activity? Perhaps during the twentieth century we were lulled into believing the church campus is the center of God's activity. As good as this is, God is on mission in the world. Churches are an instrument of God's activity, not the activity itself. Now it is time to rejoin God on mission in the world. Certainly we are the church gathered (like for worship or this Small Group), yet this is to equip us to be the church dispersed (where we spend most of our lives).

To reorient ourselves outward, making the focus of our activity the context around us, we will need to adapt. Holy Experimenting is a great pathway to walk when adapting ourselves and a community to a new reality. On Day Five this week, we were introduced to Holy Experimenting. Again, read (aloud for the group) the bulleted action steps for those who are engaging holy experimentation.

A group of people (church) who develops the ability to engage in holy experimenting is an adaptive community. What would your church need in order to engage holy experimentation? What would it need to let go; and then take hold? What might need to change within you (to make this more personal) so that you could embrace this approach to moving forward? What principles or practices might your church embrace to empower it for Holy Experimentation?

Part Three

On Day Six this week, you were invited to identify a missional engagement story from your experience. See who in the group would share a story now.

Previewing

This coming week, we will consider how consumer culture has seeped into our churches. There is nothing wrong with being consumers – this is natural and normal. But, when we look at church through the eyes of consumerism, then we encounter danger for our souls. May we grow in grace, faith and love as we engage this week's Daily Engagements.

Harvesting

God is calling each of us to join God on mission in the world. God is calling our churches to join God on mission in the world. Based on this awareness, what do you believe may be the next step for you in joining God on mission? (Do a go around)

Sending

The leader starts this prayer, then each person around the circle reads one line in turn:

Lord, make me an instrument of your peace.
Where there is hatred, let me bring love;
Where there is doubt, faith;
Where there is despair, hope;
Where there is darkness, light;
Where there is sadness, joy.
O Divine Master, grant that I may not so much seek to be consoled as to console,
To be understood as to understand,
To be loved as to love.
For it is in giving that we receive,
It is in pardoning that we are pardoned,
And it is in dying that we are born to eternal life.

Prayer of St. Francis

Leader: Through the love, grace and power of Jesus Christ our
Lord
Group: May it be so!
All: Amen!

Daily Engagements
Consumer Church

Consumer Church – Day One

"...the ultimate heresy: that we can be religious in isolation from one another,"

Robin R. Meyers
Saving Jesus From The Church

When we try living as a disciples of Jesus of Christ and joining God on mission in the world, two truths emerge in our experience. First, we are not able to sustain living in this way by ourselves. I know this is true, since I've tried going it alone. The result...epic fail. Sure, I can live the cultural Christianity I've learned through years of being immersed in church culture. Yet, I cannot sustain robust engagement, living out the teachings and lifestyle to which Christ calls by myself. It's too hard to do and sustain alone.

Second, when I am in relationship with partners intent on living in the Way of Jesus, I am more able to sustain Christ following. Experience has and is teaching me this truth. When we covenant together around shifting our lifestyles, offering mutual support and encouragement, then I make progress. When I am challenged by people who love me and are in relationship with me, then I tend to rise to the challenge. When I know these people expect the best from me, I tend to live toward their expectations. When I share a sorrow with my partners, then it becomes a half-sorrow. When I'm in faith-based partnership relationships, I am much more of a disciple of Jesus Christ.

God designed it this way. Since we are social creatures made for relationship, God provided for this need. The Church is designed to provide a community of faith with whom we can "work out our salvation." Being in relationship with other Christ-followers whose goal is to be conformed to the image of Christ, makes living in the Way of Jesus far more possible.

Praying
Thank God for those people in your life who travel along with you, fellow pilgrims on life's journey. Pray today for the disciples who are your Making The Shift Small Group. Ask God to bless them in every way today.

Sending
There are people in this world who attract you. You prefer these people when it comes to friendships. Today, identify one quality of the kinds of people you typically like, and then go about your day demonstrating that quality.

Consumer Church – Day Two

What do we mean by Consumer Church?
North American culture constantly communicates to us that we are consumers; cultivating a consumer identity. We are constantly bombarded with invitations to spend our money for this or that, whether we need it or not. Not only sellers of goods, but services also want our attention. Numerous times every day we are asked to purchase something in order to make our lives better. Over time, our identities are shaped toward seeing ourselves as consumers of goods and services.

So is it any surprise that we tend to bring this identity to our faith community experience? We tend to look through the consumer lens, evaluating our church by how well it provides religious goods and services. We go to church (rather than are the church), expecting the professionals there to deliver inspiration, training, and encouragement. We expect the church to shape our children into Christ-followers, while helping us live more satisfied lives. The bottom line for Christian consumers is whether this church delivers the goods, or not.

Is this what Jesus had in mind when he breathed the Church into being? Staying with this consumer perspective when it comes to our faith community experience leads to numerous unintended negative consequences for ourselves and the church. I believe God calls us to something different; something which has to do with Christian maturity.

Praying
Consider asking God to mature you today. Before doing so, recognize this will involve change. Are you willing to be

shaped by the Holy Spirit today?

Sending
When we deny ourselves and take up our crosses, paradoxically, we discover abundant life. As you submit your will to God's will today, go forward understanding that joy may rise up in you today.

Consumer Church – Day Three

One of the unintended negative consequences for disciples when we remain religious consumers is consumer fatigue and low brand loyalty. When one lives in a free market society with so many competing choices for one's purchasing dollar, then we grow bored with consuming the same old thing over and over. Missional practitioner Michael Frost describes how consumer fatigue plays out when it comes to church participation.

> *"Treated like consumers by the church, young Christians are abandoning the church in the same way they abandon any other product with which they get tired. In the same way that they used to be into Myspace or Facebook or online gaming or clubbing but outgrew them, they used to be into church but outgrew that as well. They have been completely and utterly immersed in this form of consumptive Christianity, and we shouldn't be surprised when they toss the church aside like their old, outmoded iPod."*

> Michael Frost
> *The Road To Missional: Journey To The Center Of The Church*

This is one aspect of life in the consumer church. We could describe other negative consequences, like immediate gratification expectations, fragile interpersonal relationships, conflict aversion, and a general stay-on-the-surface oriented faith. Obviously, this consumer identity brought to our faith is unhelpful.

Praying
Certainly we are a mixture of motivations. Consider asking God to increase your maturity when it comes to expectations for your church.

Sending
There is always someone in your faith community who could use encouragement. Today is a good day to make a call, write a note, send an email, text, or otherwise reach out to someone in your church. How about encouraging one disciple from your faith community today?

Consumer Church – Day Four

Here is the danger for not just individual disciples, but for faith communities themselves: when faith communities adopt the consumer perspective, they truncate their expression of church. Many savvy church leaders realize that church shopping is common, with prospective disciples having to choose between many options. So, they try putting the most appealing foot forward. If they adopt this marketing mindset much at all, they will channel their programs and ministries into consumer-oriented activities.

> "We exist to be an excellent provided of religious goods and services, resulting in contented members."
>
> *De facto Mission Statement*
> *of the Consumer Church*

Again, is this what Jesus had in mind for the Church? Was the goal of Jesus' ministry to create an organization which would make people feel good and not be agitated in any way? Are contented members what Jesus is looking for?

Praying
How is the Holy Spirit making you restless these days (in a positive growth-oriented way)? Where are the winds of the Spirit blowing you? Consider asking God to take you where you are needed this very day.

Sending
May you go in the fullness of the Spirit; with your cup running over today.

Consumer Church – Day Five

So how do we know how much our faith community has given itself to consumerism versus focused on faithfulness to Jesus Christ? One way to assess is to identity the questions which occupy your conversations. Contrast the two lists below.

Consumer Church Culture	*Versus*	**Sacred Partnership Communities**
How happy are our members?		What is God's calling for us as a church?
Are we doing what we can to keep our members happy?		What is God's calling for us as individuals?
How happy are our members with what this church is doing?		How well are we contributing to the development of God's disciples?
Is anyone upset, unsettled, or disgruntled?		What is needed to advance God's mission more fully; comfort or challenge?
Are there any problems we need to fix in order to restore peace?		What needs in this church are being met and what needs require attention?
How can we get people to volunteer more?		What may be holding us back from developing disciples and joining God on mission?

When the leaders (ordained and lay) of your faith community meet, which list occupies more air time? Which list tends to form the agenda? Or even in informal conversations, what's the criteria disciples in your faith community use to evaluate how well things are going? Considering our answers gives us insight into our perspectives on the nature of Church.

_____

_____

Praying
Consider praying that your church will evolve, grow, and develop to where it is collectively focused on God's kingdom rather than the church's kingdom.

Sending
Genuine and authentic life is found when we give up trying to find it. When we give ourselves to God in faith, laying down our wills; that's when we find ourselves. Identify something today which is yours by right, but which you will choose to lay down. Enjoy the freedom which results from letting go.

Consumer Church – Day Six

"Ask not what your country can do for you – ask
what you can do for your country."

John F. Kennedy
Inaugural Speech
January 20, 1961

Where do we go from here? Most of us recognize that our
faith communities are partially shaped by the consumerism in
our culture. Most of us also are not content to remain this
way. This is a time to consider our aspirations toward
Christian maturity.

John F. Kennedy challenged a nation to find its better self
through the famous statement above. You are invited to
remove the word "country," replacing it with the phrase
"faith community." This reversal quickly removes our
consumeristic tendencies, inviting us to a more balanced way
of relating in faith communities. What insights arise for you
when you consider this reversal statement?

_____

_____

_____

Praying
Consider asking God how else you might contribute to the life
of your faith community. What does your church need for
which you may be the answer?

Sending

As you go, choose to praise God today. Don't tell anyone you are doing so; instead internally know you are praising God for all the blessings in your world.

HARVESTING CONSUMER CHURCH

Gathering

Leader – Find the song "Greater," by Mercy Me on YouTube:
https://www.youtube.com/watch?v=GXI0B4iMLuU
Use a laptop, TV, Screen and projector, or whatever you have available (everyone could use their mobile devices). Watch this video together, and then, if you are bold and willing, replay it and sing along.

Share any updates you need to give this group.

Praying

Leader: We recognize, O God, that you were here before we arrived.

Group: We recognize, O God, that you are with us at all times, in all places.

Leader: Even before we made our way here, even before we moved through this day,

Group: You were here, waiting, anticipating our gathering in this place.

Leader: For you delight in your children O God.

Group: When we gather in your name and in your Spirit, you rejoice.

Leader: So now, we also rejoice in you. We reflect on our lives this week and bring these items of gratitude to you, in the presence of these sisters and brothers in Christ:

(As you are moved, speak your gratitude aloud. Pray your gratitude to God as others share)

Leader: And now, O God, we also bring our concerns, as your children, to you as our loving heavenly parent:

(As you are moved, speak your concern aloud. As you hear others share, pray their concerns to God)

Leader: And now, O God, we give you thanks for this opportunity to engage each other in life's pilgrimage.

Group: We ask that you fill us with your Holy Spirit and wrap this experience in your love.

All: Through the grace, power and love of Jesus Christ our Lord, may it be so. Amen.

Engaging

"This model (market-driven church) has a ring of truth about it. It describes only too well assumptions about membership, programs, structure, success, and purpose that give shape to today's church culture, 'the way we do things around here.' It certainly illumines the current circumstance in which the churches live, a pervasive religious consumerism driven by the quest to meet personally defined religious needs. It also explains the heavy concentration of church efforts to produce and promote programs, and it corresponds with the emphasis in one stream of literature flowing out of the church growth movement. That stream has accepted the commercial image without question by commending strategies for effectively and successfully 'marketing your church.'"

Darrell Guder
A Vision For The Sending
Of The Church In North America

"The contemporary American church is so acculturated to the American ethos of consumerism that is has little power to believe or act."

Walter Brueggeman
The Prophetic Imagination

"My point, rather, is to suggest that the church's very understanding of its purpose and mission is often shaped more obviously by the free market than by the teaching of Jesus."

Michael Frost,
The Road To Missional: Journey
To The Center Of The Church

Consumerism in church life....
Each of the above quotes describe this problematic trend. But what's actually the problem? So what if consumerism is in the church? Surely it does not directly influence how we go about what we do as churches! (Discussion Opportunity)

Results of Consumerism in church life
When we give ourselves to the consumeristic view of church life, we then make decisions about our church participation by filtering those decisions through this lens. When church leaders give in to the subtle and direct influence of

consumerism, then our churches operate with the consumer in mind. Unintended consequences follow, including these below. Talk through them, seeing if you can articulate the meaning of each. (Leaders, study this section beforehand, pages 144-52)

Low Expectation Organizations

Shallow Faith, Theology, and Discipleship

Fragile Interpersonal Relationships

Conflict Aversion

Community Tourism

Impatience – Immediate Gratification Expectations

Focus on Pleasing Constituency

Consumer Fatigue and Low Brand Loyalty

Now look back at the questions in this week's Day Five Engagement. What about your church? Look at these two contrasting lists as resting on a continuum. Where would you place the leadership of your church? Where on the continuum does your leadership spend its time and energy? If you collectively decided to move toward the "Sacred Partnership Community" questions, how would this shift how you are church together?

Remember the consumer church's mission statement: *We exist to be an excellent provider of religious goods and services, resulting in happy and content members.* This means the goal of the consumer church is to be as attractive as possible to outsiders, while keeping the members who are currently part of the church.

All of this begs the question, "Is this what Jesus had in mind?" When commissioning the disciples, through the parables, observing his ministry, listening to his teaching....Jesus did not

appear to be overly concerned about pleasing the disciples. In fact, the disciples often tried to get Jesus to tone it down, afraid he would run off potential members. Jesus described life in the kingdom as including denial of self, taking up one's cross, giving all for the pearl of great price, and laying down one's life for one's friends. We have to ask how much church-as-we-have-known-it, with varying levels of capitulation to consumer culture, is what Jesus had in mind.
(Discussion)

Previewing
There is such variety in the kinds of churches now. House churches, megachurches, biker churches, cowboy churches, traditional churches, independent churches, denominationally based churches, and even "Church Under The Bridge," (literally where it meets) are just a few. Surprisingly though, we become so immersed in our way of being church over time (remember the porcupines?) that we forget we have many options about our relationships in church. This week we will engage Sacred Partnering, another way of being in spiritual relationship together.

Harvesting
Based on today's Small Group experience, how is your understanding of being the church shifting?
(Do a go around, answering briefly)

Sending
Leader: Greater is he that is in you than he that is in the world
Group: Upon this confession (Jesus is Lord) I will build my church
Leader: And nothing in this world, or beyond it, can prevail against God's Church

Group: So we go forward with grace, peace, and power.
All: Thanks be to God! So be it! Amen!

Daily Engagements
Sacred Partnering

Sacred Partnering – Day One

What kind of faith community develops invigorated disciples who join God's movement in the world?
This question gives laser-focus to our quest for the kind of faith communities we need in this Postmodern world. When we combine the first two moves (disciple identity and missional calling), we realize we need a faith community which cultivates great spiritual vigor. Church-as-we-have-known-it may not have within it the elements needed to sustain Christ-followers in our current Postmodern world. This doesn't mean church has been wrong or bad, it simply means that church-as-we-have-known-it was designed for a different place, time, and cultural context. What's needed from faith communities now?

When faith communities engage this focal question, they are exploring *Sacred Partnering*. They are considering being in relationship with God and church, being joined together as spiritual kin. The Bible describes the relationship between Christ-followers in familial terms; brothers and sisters. What makes previously unrelated and disconnected people become nearly like family? This is something of a mystery; Holy Spirit work. We are entering the sphere of the sacred when we talk this way. Relationships evolving to this level require something beyond typical human experience - something sacred.

Not only are these relationships sacred, but they are also partnerships. As we have noted, the word "membership" has been co-opted to communicate one's relationship to an organization, which may or may not be sacred. Membership may simply be an organizational term, with organizational rights and privileges. Membership infers a transactional perspective. Partnerships though, are formed when people join themselves around a mission. Partners choose to be in relationship with one another without the quid pro quo expectations of contracts. Life partners commit to be with one another through thick and thin, good and bad, for better or worse.

Placing these two words together (Sacred Partnerships) raises the dignity, necessity, and significance of life in this 21st century faith community to new heights. Previously church relationships typically did not involve this level of participation and involvement. But previously the context of our lives was far different. Now, in order to sustain disciple identity and missional movement, we need more from each other. We need sacred partnerships.

This week we will engage five descriptions for the kinds of faith communities we need now; helping us form disciples who join in God's mission for world transformation.

Praying
Consider asking God for wisdom about your role in your faith community. Invite God to shift you if shifts are needed in how you engage your church.

Sending
As you go, may your living today bring glory to God the Father, Son, and Holy Spirit.
This is your calling, your purpose as a disciple.
May it be so. Amen.

Sacred Partnering – Day Two

"But you are a chosen race, a royal priesthood, a
holy nation, God's own people, in order that you
may proclaim the mighty acts of him who called you
out of darkness into his marvelous light. Once you
were not a people, but now you are God's people;
once you had not received mercy, but now you have
received mercy."

I Peter 2:9-10 (NRSV)

Identity Forming Faith Community
Look at all the identity-forming names Peter gives them – A
chosen race, a royal priesthood, a holy nation, God's own
people. He pulls from Jewish history and theology to
encourage identity in this new community of faith. "Once you
were not a people," Once you were not part of this faith
community; once you did not have this new identity as one of
God's people called the church. "But now you ARE God's
people." Peter encourages this new identity as one of God's
people called the church. We can imagine those early Christ-
followers who experienced the great dispersion soon after
the resurrection...having to move away from their
communities of origin, becoming geographical nomads due to
persecution and prejudice, hearing those sweet
words..."Once you were not a people, but now you are God's
people." Now they are part of the Beloved Community.
Thanks be to God.

But now you ARE God's people....
Sit with this identity marker a few moments. Recognize
yourself. You are one of God's people. You are invited to

embrace this identity deep down in your bones. As you do so, what does it mean to you?

_____

_____

_____

Praying

The Holy Spirit is given to you as a seal; a confirmation of your identity as a child of God.

Pray that God will eliminate any doubt in your soul that you are God's own.

Sending

Go now, and as you go, know that YOU ARE one of God's people!

May you live your identity this very day.

Sacred Partnering – Day Three

Geographical Anchoring Faith Community
During the twentieth century, the suburban lifestyle was born, with the church quickly adapting. Disciples were more transient, coming and going depending on their job assignments and opportunities. Disciples were also more mobile. They were conditioned to travel distances to work (suburbs to the city), so they transferred this experience to their church life. Churches then became more regional. They were "outsourced" from neighborhoods to more of a franchise model (like all the other consumer oriented organizations around them). Some even developed satellites of their franchises in other suburban communities.

Now in the 21st century we are seeing the reverse of these trends. People are moving from the suburb to the city. "Go local" is now common language. We are recognizing ourselves as tourists in our own communities, hardly attached to place at all. This has created a strong hunger in humankind for place; for a place to call home. Postmodern Christ-followers hunger for a faith community which is deeply rooted in its place on the planet, forming a strong bond with its local community.

The opportunity this presents to the 21st century church is to "go local." The Postmodern church can serve as an anchoring community. We already see our church communities as spiritually and relationally anchoring for us. We become the church gathered for worship and Christian formation. This anchors our faith and fuels our spiritual tanks for being the church dispersed. Postmodern churches can become anchors in another very tangible way. Those faith communities with buildings are identified with a particular place in their community. It is time to see the church (people and building) as a part of that community, as a part of the local culture. In order to live as invigorated disciples in our current context, we need church to grow connected to place. We need our churches to embrace the local, investing in its community context, being a part of and contributing to the shaping of our local contexts. This will help anchor Postmodern Christ-followers in the 21st century.

And here you are, living in this particular community. Why you, here? What's your purpose or calling for being in this community at this time? As you reflect, what comes to you?

_____

_____

_____

Praying
Today, O God, show me how I can be salt and light right where I am.
Today, O God, help me to engage those around me, expressing your love as I go.

Sending
Go now, and as you go, may you express the grace of God which your community is dying to receive.

Sacred Partnering – Day Four

"From now on, therefore, we regard no one from a
human point of view; even though we once knew
Christ from a human point of view, we know him no
longer in that way. So if anyone is in Christ, there is a
new creation: everything old has passed away; see,
everything has become new!"

2 Corinthians 5:16-18 (NRSV)

Personal Transformation Faith Community

What kind of faith community cultivates or incubates
disciples who are personally growing and being transformed
by the Spirt of God? What role do sacred partnerships play in
helping this new creation blossom and bloom? How shall we
relate to one another when we want to encourage this kind
of personal transformation in each other? This is not quick
work. Personal transformation toward the reflection of Jesus
Christ is the long slow work of salvation. This is sanctification
work, to use a theological word. We need communities of
faith who can engage disciples in this work with patient
intentionality, knowing this journey takes a lifetime to
complete.

"It seems only fair, for example, to ask that the
members of the body of Christ look and act
differently from those who are not part of the
beloved community. They should seem like 'resident
aliens,' according to authors Stanley Hauerwas and
William H. Willimon, a part of a 'colony' more than a
congregation. The Christian community should not

feel at home in the world, as if it is a 'voluntary organization of like-minded individuals.'"

Robin R. Meyers
Saving Jesus From The Church

You are in the process of becoming a disciple. What may be yours to let go and lay aside? What may be yours to take hold and start doing?

_____
_____
_____

Praying
Lord God, there are parts of myself...habits, perspectives, indulgences...which I do not want to let go or stop doing. I like them, though I know they shrink my life and hold me back. I need your help O God; I need your help to let these go. So, into your hands I commit these things. Liberate me I pray. Cleanse me and put a new and right spirit within me. Amen.

Sending
Receive the grace and peace of the Lord. Know that through the blood and love of Jesus Christ, you are redeemed. Now go, living as if you are freshly born. Embrace this day like a slave who is just now set free. Thanks be to God.

Sacred Partnering – Day Five

Thy kingdom come, thy will be done on earth as it is in heaven.

Jesus Christ
Matthew's Gospel

World Transformation Faith Community

When we pray this prayer, we are joining with God's mission to bring the kingdom of God to earth as it is in heaven. What a radical prayer. And, a somewhat radical faith community is required to cultivate this kind of Christ-follower. This kind of faith community is on mission with God, focused on cultivating no less than world transformation. This faith community believes the world is not as it should be in its current expression, but it is not yet what it shall be in its transformed kingdom expression. This faith community is on mission with God in this world, engaging in world transformation.

We have already explored how personal transformation is part of the Christian movement's purpose. As we are being transformed personally, we are called to participate in God's transformation of the world. This includes addressing the structures, policies, practices of our society. This is participation in the public square, addressing the large scale injustices in our society. Poverty, Racism, Earth Stewardship...these and many other issues need the Christian voice as part of the dialogue.

These, and many other Postmodern Era issues, call the Church to join God's mission to bring the kingdom to earth as it is in heaven. We are called to work for our personal transformation, while also joining God in world transformation.

How do you feel about this part of Christ-following; the call to work for justice? Realizing this kind of discipleship leads us into issues which are emotionally charged and politically loaded, what do we need from one another in our faith communities in order to strengthen our resolve in these areas?

_____

_____

_____

Praying
O God, your call includes a call to maturity. Sometimes I don't want to "grow-up" in my faith. I rather just cruise along, being nominally involved in this Christian movement. Change me, grow me, empower me to step up and grow up. May I follow you into working for systemic change in our world even today. Amen.

Sending
Go now in the awareness that you are part of God's plan to change the world.
Go now, collaborating with God, partnering with God, toward the kingdom's actualization on earth, like it is in heaven. You (through the grace of God) can do this. Go.

Sacred Partnering – Day Six

Partnership Pilgrimage Faith Community

Did we save the best description of a new kind of faith community for last? Well, it seems like it's extremely important. By now you know that I am clear on my inability to sustain living in the Way of Jesus on my own. There is no doubt in my mind, nor in my experience, that I must have travelling partners to sustain this pilgrimage. Yes, there are times when we take a stand alone. Yet those times are very rare. We human beings are social creatures who function best when part of a significant community with supportive ties.

Jesus seemed to encourage strong relational connections in the body of Christ. During the Farewell Discourse, Jesus gives the new commandment we discussed earlier.

> "Little children, I am with you only a little longer. You will look for me; and as I said to the Jews so now I say to you, 'Where I am going, you cannot come.' I give you a new commandment, that you love one another. Just as I have loved you, you also should love one another. By this everyone will know that you are my disciples, if you have love for one another."
>
> *John 13:33-35 (NRSV)*

Clearly, the way to determine whether we are disciples, according to this passage, is how we love one another in the Body of Christ (church). When lived, this new commandment leads to close relational connections among Christ's disciples;

sacred partnerships. Now, compare this description to your experience in your church. What insights arise for you?

_____

_____

_____

Praying
Lord God, I am the church. This means I actively create and shape the church as I go. Help me, O God, to love more, criticize less, forgive fast, and bring out the best in my sacred partners today.

Sending
Go now, knowing that your sacred partners need you. They need you to love and encourage them toward being disciples. Look for specific opportunities today to be church to other disciples.

HARVESTING SACRED PARTNERING

Gathering

What is it?

What is it about this particular church; this community of faith, that you choose to be a part of it? There are many churches in North America, yet you choose to be part of this one. Why this one? Do a go around, sharing one answer each to this question.

Praying

Leader: We recognize, O God, that you were here before we arrived.

Group: We recognize, O God, that you are with us at all times, in all places.

Leader: Even before we made our way here, even before we moved through this day,

Group: You were here, waiting, anticipating our gathering in this place.

Leader: For you delight in your children O God.

Group: When we gather in your name and in your Spirit,

you rejoice.

Leader: So now, we also rejoice in you. We reflect on our lives this week and bring these items of gratitude to you, in the presence of these sisters and brothers in Christ:
(As you are moved, speak your gratitude aloud. Pray your gratitude to God as others share)

Leader: And now, O God, we also bring our concerns, as your children, to you as our loving heavenly parent:
(As you are moved, speak your concern aloud. As you hear others share, pray their concerns to God)

Leader: And now, O God, we give you thanks for this opportunity to engage each other in life's pilgrimage.
Group: We ask that you fill us with your Holy Spirit and wrap this experience in your love.
All: Through the grace, power and love of Jesus Christ our Lord, may it be so. Amen.

Engaging
What kind of faith community develops invigorated disciples who join God's movement in the world?
This is the pivotal, primary question when it comes to designing how we relate with one another in God's Church. This is the question which can guide how we organize ourselves, how we staff our churches, and most everything we do.

Caution: Disciples in churches will find this question mildly interesting, or even peripheral, until they try living fully as disciples plus joining God on mission. This is why this third big move (Sacred Partnering) is sequentially last. When we try living in the Way of Jesus, engaging the first two big moves, then the realization that we cannot do it alone become crystal clear.

So, now let's draw these three big moves together. When we want to become disciples in deep, robust ways...when we want to join God's movement in the world, making a difference, and collaborating with kingdom movement....then what do we need from each other to support this kind of living?

Activity: Your Group Leader will record your insights on a large surface where you can see them.
First, in popcorn fashion, share one insight about what you need from each other in order to live the way we are describing. This is about relationships and community within your church.
Second, consider other aspects of being church together. What do you need from the church which could empower and equip you to live this way?
Third, what would need to change about your perspective, attitude, and involvement with your church in order for the first and second items above to actually happen?

Now, look at these lists and reflect on these insights. How do you feel about this? Are these promising directions for your church to move? How ready are you for this kind of deep, robust community of faith engagement? (Discuss your reactions and responses)

Covenant
Throughout history humankind has used covenants to give shape and direction to relationships. Sometimes these are very formal, like wedding vows. Other times they are less

formal, like signing the agreement about how your swim team will function. So, what might be included in a covenant which guides your church relationships and participation? What would you ask disciples to bring to their faith community involvement? What could each disciple contribute to answering the pivotal, primary question above?

Group Leader: To "prime the pump" you may want to read aloud the "Marks Of A New Monasticism" found in Appendix 4, p.221 in *Shift*.

(Discuss and list)

Previewing

God loves us just as we are. God loves us unconditionally. This means we don't have to improve or shape up before God accepts us. God loves us...period. It is just as true that God also believes we can become more than we currently are as people. In fact, God has given us gifts, talents, and assets which are needed in the world. God actually has a calling for each of us; part of God's mission in which we can partner with God. So, calling is not about our essential worth or acceptability in God's eyes. Calling is about what we do in response to God's great love.

This week we will engage the concept of calling, considering our callings for this season of life.

Harvesting

Sacred Partnering. Do a go around wherein you are invited to complete this sentence:

When I consider my involvement in Sacred Partnering through this church, I _____.

Sending

There is no doubt – you ARE God's people. So go now, knowing you are part of this holy tribe. Go now, in the awareness that once you were no people, but now you are the community of saints. Go now, living in sacred partnerships with those right here in this room, and in your larger faith community. Come alive friends, to the beloved community of which you are a very significant part. Amen.

Daily Engagements
Calling

Calling – Day One

Member Identity to Disciple Identity
Attractional Church to Missional Church
Consumer Church to Sacred Partnering

What a journey we are engaging...moving from the Modern Era (last 500 years) to the Postmodern Era (unknown territory). We are moving from church-as-we-have-known-it to church-as-it-is-becoming. We are living in the greatest transitional time of our lifetimes thus far. Everything around us is changing.

Simultaneously, God is creating again, bringing substance from chaos. These three Spirit-inspired moves of God's Church are flowing. During this week we will engage various activities which will help us harvest our gains during this Making The Shift experience. To get us started, pause and reflect on your experience. What have you gained through the Small Group gatherings and these Daily Engagements? By identifying your answers to this question, you will preserve your insights while they are fresh. Also, by writing them out, you will capture and integrate them more readily. So, what have you gained?

_____

_____

_____

Praying
God's mercies are new every morning. God's grace is fresh every day. Consider asking God to help you live like a more mature disciple than you currently believe you are. Then

your self-perception will expand to accommodate your expansive living.

Sending

Holy experimenting is trying something new which we believe may be consistent with God's calling. Today engage the holy experiment described above in "Praying," moving out in faith.

Calling – Day Two

We are working out our salvation day by day, becoming more who God is calling us to become.

We will complete this task when the end of all things comes, and not before. Yes, we are works in progress. We are seeking progress, not perfection. Given this, you are invited to evaluate your progress toward making the Shifts. Please rate each Shift below on a 0-10 scale. Zero means you are not even started, making no progress. Ten means you are moving extremely fast, progressing by leaps and bounds.

1. Member Identity to Disciple Identity _____
2. Attractional Church to Missional Church_____
3. Consumer Church to Sacred Partnering_____

Now, let's identify what is helping and what is hindering your growth.

- Identify your highest rating above, which indicates an area of strength for you. What are you doing which is contributing to your growth in this area?

  _____

  _____

  Now, consider how you might do more of what's helping you make this progress.

- Identify your lowest rating above, which indicates a growth area for you. What are you doing,

thinking, engaging which may be holding you back
regarding this Shift?

_____

_____

Now, consider what you might do to address
what's holding you back.

Praying
Consider praying that God will help you shift to another
way of life; to greater discipleship.

Sending
Time flies! So as you go today, go ahead and embrace your
calling to be salt and light. There is no time like the
present. Fulfill your calling, one day at a time, including
this day.

Calling – Day Three

We don't go to church; we are the church, everywhere and at all times. Since our faith communities are groups of real live human beings, they too are works in progress. You are invited to rate your faith community just like you rated yourself yesterday on this 0-10 scale. Zero means your church is not even started, making no progress. Ten means your church is moving extremely fast, progressing by leaps and bounds.

1. Member Identity to Disciple Identity _____
2. Attractional Church to Missional Church_____
3. Consumer Church to Sacred Partnering_____

Now, let's identify what is helping and what is hindering.

- Identify your church's highest rating above, which indicates an area of strength. What is your church doing which is contributing to growth in this area?

_____

_____

   Now, consider how your church might do more of what's helping make this progress.

- Identify your church's lowest rating above. What might be holding your church back regarding this Shift? _____

_____

   Now, consider what your church might do to address what's holding the church back.

Praying

Perhaps you are taking note of your contribution to the slowness or reluctance of your church moving ahead. If so, consider laying your reluctance at Jesus' feet. Ask God if God wants you to pick it back up or leave it there.

Sending

There are people in your community who do not have a faith community. They will know you are a Christian by your love. Try to do something so loving today that someone asks you why you did it.

Calling – Day Four

Perhaps it's time.
Perhaps it's time to give ourselves permission.
Perhaps it's time to give ourselves permission to quit
church-as-we-have-known-it.
Perhaps it's time to give ourselves permission to quit
church-as-we-have-known-it so that we can engage
church-as-it-is-becoming.
Perhaps it's time to become Church powered by
renewable energy sources;
Holy Spirit Wind.

Can we grant ourselves this kind of permission? Will we
exercise courage, letting go the trapeze bar, flying forward
toward a new way of being church? It's funny how this
faith journey happens. Often in my own experience, and
that of my family, we find our way only after we are willing
to let go of our former way. I guess that's what faith is
about. Faith is what we do when we let go without yet
knowing where we are going. Faith is leaving what we
know for the land we-know-not-of. May we be found faith-
full. May we be captivated by a yearning for God's wide,
boundless ocean.

Praying
What might you need to let go? God will help, if you ask.

Sending
When we let go, we often find great relief. We were
carrying burdens or expectations which were heavy. As
you go, breathe easier, allowing yourself to enjoy the relief
of letting go.

Calling – Day Five

"If you want to build a ship, don't summon people
to buy wood, prepare tools, distribute jobs, and
organize the work, rather teach people the
yearning for the wide, boundless ocean."

Antoine de Saint-Exupery

The work of the Holy Spirit....
Making these three big moves in and through our faith
communities is a calling which some cannot deny. After
this, some will not be content returning to church-as-we-
have-known-it, having discovered a yearning for
something more. This is where the Holy Spirit meets us - at
the edge of our comfort zone, glimpsed in our peripheral
vision, calling in the middle of the night, teasing our souls
with a still small voice, enticing us into the dark which
becomes light after the courageous first step. So what
now? Follow the Spirit's call. Trust your faith journey.
Move ahead. Give into that longing. Were you to do so,
these are possible next steps:

_____
_____
_____

Praying
When we taste of the Lord, we find that the Lord is good.
Remember the pearl of great price and the treasure buried
in the field? God wants you to enjoy the goodness of the
Lord. Open yourself now to God's good gifts through
prayer.

Sending

Now go forth into this world, living out of the spiritual invigoration which comes from connection with your Lord.

Calling – Day Six

For Longing
A Blessing From John O'Donohue, found in *To Bless The Space Between Us*

Blessed be the longing that brought you here and quickens your soul with wonder.
May you have the courage to listen to the voice of desire that disturbs you when you have settled for something safe.
May you have the wisdom to enter generously into your own unease to discover the new direction your longing wants you to take.
May the forms of your belonging – in love, creativity, and friendship – be equal to the grandeur and call of your soul.
May the one you long for long for you.
May your dreams gradually reveal the destination of your desire.
May a secret Providence guide your thought and nurture your feeling.
May your mind inhabit your life with the sureness with which your body inhabits the world.
May your heart never be haunted by ghost-structures of old damage.
May you come to accept your longing as divine urgency.
May you know the urgency with which God longs for you.

Through the grace, power, and love of Jesus Christ our Lord, may it be so.

Praying
Read over the blessing above again, listening for the lines

which are especially for you today. Then lift them in prayer
to God, trusting God to know their importance for your
journey.

Sending
You too have the power to bless or curse. There are people
in your world who need your blessing, or any blessing.
Look for them as you go today, offering a word of hope
and blessing to those who come across your pathway.

HARVESTING CALLING

Gathering

Jesus was called to live out his mission.

Group Leader, find the song and video on youtube.com entitled "How He Loves," by John Mark McMillan; pictures – "40" by Si Smith. Show this video in some way to this Small Group.

Share any updates or news you want your Small Group to know.

Praying

Leader: We recognize, O God, that you were here before we arrived.

Group: We recognize, O God, that you are with us at all times, in all places.

Leader: Even before we made our way here, even before we moved through this day,

Group: You were here, waiting, anticipating our gathering in this place.

Leader: For you delight in your children O God.

Group: When we gather in your name and in your Spirit,

you rejoice.

Leader: So now, we also rejoice in you. We reflect on our lives this week and bring these items of gratitude to you, in the presence of these sisters and brothers in Christ:
(As you are moved, speak your gratitude aloud. Pray your gratitude to God as others share)

Leader: And now, O God, we also bring our concerns, as your children, to you as our loving heavenly parent:
(As you are moved, speak your concern aloud. As you hear others share, pray their concerns to God)

Leader: And now, O God, we give you thanks for this opportunity to engage each other in life's pilgrimage.
Group: We ask that you fill us with your Holy Spirit and wrap this experience in your love.
All: Through the grace, power and love of Jesus Christ our Lord, may it be so. Amen.

Engaging
Calling. Every Christ-follower; every church...we are each called to participate with God in unveiling the kingdom here on earth. This week we engaged this Christian concept, exploring our personal and congregational calling.

Look at Day 5 together, spending some time here. Group Leader, facilitate a go around on each of the three big moves, recording the numbers. Then, lead the group to step back and reflect on what these numbers mean. Share your insights about your faith community rising up through this reflection.

Now, move to the strengths and weaknesses. Someone

share a strength (high number) and see how many others also identified that strength. Discuss what you do as a church which makes this a strength and what you might do to strengthen this even more. Repeat the same process for the weaknesses (lower number).

Does the progress stop here? This Making The Shift Small Group is drawing to a close. We hope that you will continue making these shifts in your personal spiritual journey. In addition, we hope your church will continue these movements also. Spend some time discussing what may be your next steps as a congregation.

Harvesting
I am, and will be different, because of this Small Group experience in this way _____ .

Sending
Now, as you go, know that you ARE God's people.
God's creative Spirit brought you into this world.
God's power sustains you to this very moment.
So go now, and be who you are in Christ.
Go as salt, to flavor this world. Go as light, to shine in the darkness.
Go as grace, to bring healing and hope to this broken and hurting world.
And may the peace of God, which surpasses all comprehension, guard our hearts and minds in Christ Jesus until we meet again.
Amen.

EPILOGUE

The clean and healthy food movement is underway in North America. First came a keen interest in eating a more healthy diet. People recognized our bodies naturally crave healthy, life-giving foods which provide what we need to function well. For some, it's difficult to recognize our desire for healthy foods, since we have trained our physical systems to crave sugar or fat-based foods. Only after a detoxing experience, partnered with retraining our palates, do we rediscover a taste for healthy foods. Once we develop a taste for the good stuff, we recognize the lack of nutrition in unhealthy foods.

During this Making The Shift Small Group experience, I hope this spiritual detoxing, cleansing, and rediscovery process has taken hold with you. The Apostle Peter describes the process well.

> "So clean house! Make a clean sweep of malice and pretense, envy and hurtful talk. You've had a taste of God. Now, like infants at the breast, drink deep of God's pure kindness. Then you'll grow up mature and whole in God."
>
> *I Peter 2:1-3, The Message*

When we taste of the Lord, we find that the Lord is good. Our spiritual appetites are activated; our taste buds reoriented. Now we want the good stuff. Now we are launched on this journey as disciples who join God's mission, supported by a robust faith community. There is no way we want to stop this movement.

So what now for you and your small group?
Many faith communities are ready to go deeper...shifting their priorities and culture toward these three big moves. Some of these are working with (or can start now) a Making The Shift Coach who is guiding the next step. Others are pursuing this movement on their own. Either way, your small group has identified many insights about living out these three big moves in your context. These are extremely valuable when it comes to discerning the next steps. If your faith community is working with a coach, you already know who will receive your insights. If not, ask and find out where your input goes. The goal here is to continue the shift, engaging these three big moves at the highest level...as a church.

Our design for the Making The Shift Process includes establishing three teams who receive this input. They are tasked with identifying the foreseeable steps for implementing these three moves. After a brief work period, these three teams coordinate with the leadership and entire congregation, resulting in your Making The Shift Plan. This is not a traditional planning process, being far more simple. This is a discernment activity, harvesting the insights from the small groups, and identifying pathways ahead. Then faith communities have actionable direction for continuing this journey and culture shift.

Thank you for participating in this Making The Shift Small Group Experience. Please feel free to reach out to us at Pinnacle Leadership Associates if we can assist you as you pursue God's calling. May we each become who we are (disciples), joining God on mission (missional movement), while partnering with faithful travelling companions (sacred partnering).

Mark Tidsworth
President
Pinnacle Leadership Associates

To receive our weekly e-newsletter, which includes articles on these things, sign-up on our website at
www.pinnaclelead.com/contact
Facebook Page: Pinnacle Leadership Associates and Mark Tidsworth
803-673-3634
markt@pinnaclelead.com